Shattered

HOW TO BREAK THROUGH WHAT'S HOLDING YOU BACK AND OPEN UP A LIFE OF GOD'S GREATNESS

Dianne Wyper

DIANNE WYPER

UNITED HOUSE

Published by UNITED HOUSE Publishing

ISBN-13: 978-1-7327194-5-3

UNITED HOUSE Publishing
Waterford, Michigan
info@unitedhousepublishing.com
www.unitedhousepublishing.com

Cover and interior design: Matt Russell, Marketing Image, mrussell@marketing-image.com
Back cover photography: Meg Lince, megolincephotography.com

Printed in the United States of America
2019—First Edition

Dedicated to the best guy in the whole world.

"Bye, love ya, see ya!"

CONTENTS

FOREWORD 7

INTRODUCTION. 11

Chapter 1: I Had a Vision 17

Chapter 2: Yup, I Yelled at God 27

Chapter 3: Unmerited Favor 37

Chapter 4: Sickness, Debt, and Notecards 47

Chapter 5: Cliffs, Ladders, and Jail Cells 71

Chapter 6: Movies and the Bathroom Stall. 87

Chapter 7: Being Authentically You 95

Chapter 8: Getting Hung Up 111

Chapter 9: Sailing the Sea 133

Chapter 10: Get out of the Doorway. 145

THAT'S A WRAP! 159

ACKNOWLEDGEMENTS. 165

ABOUT THE AUTHOR 169

FOREWORD

There are two types of people: extinguishers and igniters. Extinguishers are those who carry water, and people in this category have been known to put out the fire of your dreams, leaving them nothing more than a disappointing pile of wet ashes. But, igniters? These are the rare few who carry fuel and pour it on to the spark of your idea, turning it into a blazing wildfire, lighting up the path to the life of your dreams.

We'd all do well to surround ourselves with people who throw fuel on our dreams, not attempt to drown them out.

Dianne Wyper is an igniter. Our paths first crossed while we were both searching for our church home. We quickly became friends as we learned we both loved to read, we love Jesus, listening to sermons, going to church conferences, and of course, we are coffee fanatics—I mean that last one was *really* what sealed the deal for me. Ha! But I have discovered that one of the most beautiful qualities about my friend Dianne is: she's a dreamer. She believes we can dream big because our God is big; we can expect big, miraculous things for our lives.

In *Shattered*, Dianne shares her journey of learning that with God great things really are possible. She isn't sharing this from a "I hope this could be true" point of view. She can speak about God's greatness because she lives it.

Her life was completely turned upside down by God when He shattered the lies she'd believed and stepped into true freedom. From miraculous healing to financial provision, to brand-new confidence, joy, peace, forgiveness, and love—Dianne has experienced it all, and as her friend, I've watched her live out this message.

I'm honored to introduce you to my friend—your guide through the pages of this book and in the journey towards receiving every single gift God has for you. If there is anything I've learned about stepping into your calling and chasing your dream, is that first, you need to identify and overcome the obstacles which are keeping you from pursuing it. It is time to shatter every barrier which has prevented you from God's best and step into the greatest life you've ever known. If you're willing to give her a chance, my friend Dianne may ignite the dream which lies in your heart.

Amber Olafsson
Author of *THE AWESOME ONE*

INTRODUCTION

We are officially the owners of an in-ground pool, and for months, I've been made aware of an upcoming cannonball contest. In all honesty, I'm not a cannonball kind of girl. I like to stick my toes in and test the water first. Are you with me? This momma ain't gettin' in no cold pool.

But like so many other things, the pull of adventure beckons my heart to answer its call. I often question if it's truly adventure or only pure craziness, but nonetheless, I love it. I don't always say yes to its echoing invitation, but when I do, I'm thankful I did.

I guess you could say I've realized this whole adventure thing is a gift. One that is quite beautiful both to watch and experience. Sadly, the older I get, the more often I let that gift sit all wrapped up with a nice little bow because I'm too comfortable to partake.

I've learned that just like my kids beg me to cannonball with them physically, God beckons me to quit testing the waters and get a running start for the cannonball experience of a lifetime. He's challenging me, and He's challenging you, too. The call is for us to simply go for it, to dive into all He has for us.

Let me explain. Recently, God has surrounded me with people who are spiritually cannonballing left and right, and in the meantime, splashing me with all their frolicking, fun, spiritual water.

There I sat on the side, in my nice little cover-up, towel in hand to keep myself as dry as possible, sipping my La' Croix and enjoying my little space, my comfort. But, after watching those jumping left and right, what I noticed was my soul began to crave what they had. I wanted to be like them. They carried a confidence in God that was different. Somehow, they were fearless; they were joyful and expectant that the pool, the opportunity in front of them, was one they were not going to miss. They were so excited about it that they didn't waste their time testing the waters. They simply went for it; they jumped. For the first time in my life, I began to get uncomfortable with my comfort. I couldn't sit on the edge of the spiritual pool any longer. There was something calling me; God was calling me. I knew it was time to put the comfort behind me and go for it. So, I took a step, I ran, and I jumped!

Are you a cannonball person? Are you the person who just goes for it? Have you ever decided to go all in and just do it? I'm not talking about sticking your toe in; I mean flat out jumping all in. Most won't do it. Most won't jump. Why you ask? Because it's crazy, wild, exhilarating, and adventurous with no guarantee of what's to come. The majority won't put aside the what-ifs, the fears, or the thoughts of others and just go for it. That was me. I really enjoyed my comfort, and while staying cozy in my convenience, I secretly worried about other people's opinions. In all honesty, it's still a bit of a struggle, but I'm learning not to worry if others approve of my crazy cannonballing or whether I splash them in the process. I'm learning not to worry about what I look like as I jump or stress about whether the water is shockingly cold.

I've been chained to fear and what-ifs, worried about the opinions of others for far too long. Anyone with me? This life is an adventure. It's a journey; it's a gift, and if we stay stuck in fear, we're going to stay camped out at the Motel 8 and miss out on the grand resort that's scheduled to be the next destination. We must remember, there is always a next stop.

That's one of the things I love so much about following Jesus. He always has the next step for each of us, and it doesn't matter what people's opinions are of our walk. What matters is that we listen, move, jump, and do!

Every fresh adventure and every new stop holds different lessons and beautiful gifts to unwrap.

Throughout these pages, I'll share parts of my journey—my adventure. Over the past few years, I've asked some tough questions, and the truths God has revealed to me have meshed together in the following pages. His truth, His spoken word over me has completely changed my world. It's ridiculous how simple yet profound He makes things. I hope you will join me on an adventure of a lifetime. Jumping from cliffs, experiencing rare forms of beauty, breaking down walls, shattering fears and insecurities, unwrapping gifts you could only dream of, cannonballing, and even crying in a few bathroom stalls. It's all here, the journey of how I learned that I am gifted beyond measure, and so are you. You'll learn what's waiting for you, how to find it, take it, apply it, and use it. Together we will learn that it's okay to expect God's greatness. Then, we'll learn how to speak it, believe it, and experience it. Get ready to celebrate, friends. Walls are about to fall, and you're about to dive into the most lavish spread you could have ever imagined.

I pray that these pages speak life into your soul. My prayer is that these wouldn't merely be words from my heart, but that the King of Kings and the Lord of Lords would whisper His truth to you. That you would see His words come alive in a new way because they will shatter life as you know it; they are life-changing.

I can't wait to see what He has for you.

Come on, let's jump!

1

I Had a Vision

THE VISION THAT CHANGED EVERYTHING

Have you ever had a dream or a thought that was so real, it was as if you were actually there experiencing the sounds, the emotions, and the excitement of it all?

Just the other day, I put my hand on my son Braden's shoulder to wake him, and after a few nudges, he yelled, "Mom! Why did you wake me up? I was playing in the Super Bowl!" He was so frustrated with me. His anger seeped out of his little sleepy voice as he said, "Now I'm never gonna know if we won."

I'm not sure if Braden's team would have won or lost the Super Bowl in his dream that morning, but what I do know is what it's like to experience a dream, a vision, or a thought that is so real, it's as if it's being played out right before your eyes. So real it seems tangible, touchable.

It was just a few years ago I experienced this.

It was a moment when layers were peeled back, and blinders fell from my eyes, and I realized I had a very jaded viewpoint on personal freedom. It will forever be etched into the depths of my heart and mind. It's a moment that changed my perspective of something very vital. I want you to join me and step into what it was that I saw that day, a vision that God Himself used to change my life and understanding of what it means to be His.

It was a typical day, nothing extraordinary planned for the morning. I did what I normally do on days like that. My husband had just left for work, so I grabbed my cup of coffee and sat with my Bible and notebook. I was doing what most moms of littles do, get their alone time in before the kiddos wake.

I don't even remember what I was reading that morning, but what I do remember is what happened during my prayer time.

As I sat at my dining room table praying, something different occurred. Typically, I pray with my eyes shut, and it's, well, dark. But, during this prayer, that changed. God showed me something amazing.

As I began to pray, my surroundings completely transformed before me. With my eyes closed tight, the darkness suddenly turned to light, and I was in a room. It was just a room, but the most beautiful one I have ever seen. I found myself standing in the middle of this box of beauty. Now, I didn't actually go anywhere, but it's as if I was there, standing in this outrageously gorgeous space. It was so magnificent. I can hardly find words to describe it.

I'm an atmosphere junkie. I love beautiful spaces. Places that are warm, inviting, beautifully decorated, filled with warmth and love.

But this surpassed anything I have ever experienced with my own eyes. It was absolutely breathtaking.

My emotions may have been enhanced because of how I felt while I was there. The joy I felt from being in this room transcended any earthly experience I've ever had. Not only was it stunning, but I was overflowing with peace and wonder. Words cannot do it justice.

As I began to take a few steps forward, I became filled with an overwhelming excitement of what I saw; something I'd never seen in all my life. At the front of this room was the most beautiful, ornate banquet table I had ever seen. *Fixer Upper* ain't got nothin' on this room or this table. It was fit for a queen if you will. This table stretched across the whole front of the room. It was massive, the most enormous table imaginable. It just kept going.

It may seem crazy that I'm emphasizing how exquisite this table was, but it was breathtaking. Stunning, gold, and shimmering. This gorgeous table was overflowing with something even more magnificent, something so precious that my mind could not even begin to comprehend. Hanging over the edges and cascading all along the front and sides of this table were gifts, but not just any gifts. These were the most beautifully wrapped packages my eyes had ever beheld. They were stacked, staggered, and covering every square inch of space this table had to offer. The presents were too many to count, too dazzling for words to describe, and I didn't even know what was in them.

The table's lavishness drew me closer. As I made my way toward it, trying to take everything in, I noticed a detail that I'll never forget. Every one of these gifts had my name on them (spelled correctly, too). Now mind you, this was not the typical birthday or Christmas spread. This was different, special. But why? For what? What was this all about?

After observing for a few moments, I moved forward to grab a gift; how could I resist? But just as I reached my arm out, *BAM!!!* I hit something.

I tried again but was stopped a second time.

I stepped back, and from floor to ceiling, side to side, I noticed a barrier wall as clear as one could imagine. I wouldn't have noticed it if I hadn't hit it time and time again, trying to take what was clearly laid out for me. And, just as quickly as it had started, suddenly, the vision was done. It was over. I opened my eyes and immediately wrote every detail down. I was sobbing, overwhelmed with whatever it was I had just experienced. This was a first for me. I'd never been shown something so beautiful and unique. I was confused but in a curious way. What did I just see? This dream, this vision, whatever it was, consumed my mind for the days, weeks, and months to follow.

I asked God about a hundred times a day during the week that followed what the experience was all about, but I heard nothing in response. He let me ponder on it, think about it, wonder, dream.

A few months later, I was doing some work around the house, and my thoughts became consumed with the words, "Break it down, break it down." I tried to blow it off, thinking maybe they were simply lyrics from a song or something. I had no clue why I would suddenly think the phrase *break it down, break it down*. God wasn't going to let me brush it off for long. The words grew intensely strong, and suddenly what came to my mind brought me to my knees, weeping on my kitchen floor.

I closed my eyes and began to see that room again. Everything was exactly the same as before, everything but the wall. This time the glass barricade wasn't so transparent. This time my wall was covered in words, dark heavy words. Even now, tears flood my eyes just reminiscing about it. It was dreadful. As I began to read through them, I realized very quickly exactly what it was. It was me! There it was written out, my identity, the way I saw myself, and it was sad. The words were a mix of actions of others that I had allowed to shape and mold me, past regrets, shame, hurt, rejection, and fear. I saw words that represented the choices I had made and had allowed to become my identity. These were things I kept deep down, many things no one knew but me.

There it stood, this wall of ugly standing in front of me, preventing me from receiving all God had for me.

It wasn't easy to see; it hurt. Standing face to face with things I've allowed to label me and shape me hurt. I would never speak those words over another human being on the planet. Why had I spoken them over my life?

I don't believe this experience was for me alone, I know I am supposed to share it with others. Too many of us are barricaded by walls of defeat. We're silenced, chained, and distracted. The Bible says in 1 Peter 5:8 that the Devil walks around like a roaring lion seeking those whom he may devour. For me, the enemy used words. He

FOR ME, THE ENEMY USED WORDS. HE USED OTHERS AND EVEN MYSELF TO SPEAK DEFEAT AND DESTRUCTION OVER MY LIFE.

used others and even myself to speak defeat and destruction over my life. Over time, I began to agree with him. I started to believe those things to be true. I had allowed an extremely dangerous thing to happen. I had made some agreements with the enemy, and little by little, word by word, thought by thought, he was defeating me, devouring me. The vision God gave me changed all of that. God allowed me to see what was happening, what I had been doing. Through His unending love, grace, and mercy, He taught me how to break those agreements, and day by day, step by step, God began to restore my life in a way that only He could.

So, friends, I ask you, what's on your wall?

SO, FRIENDS, I ASK YOU, WHAT'S ON YOUR WALL?

Is it covered with things from your past? Is there shame, regret, hurt, rejection, what-ifs, lies, slander, unbelief, gossip? Are there words like "unworthiness," "undeserving," "unloved"? Maybe it's not your past but your present, and your wall is covered with things like "lost," "purposeless," "trapped," "confused." Could it be the actions of others: abandonment, abuse, lies, broken dreams? Maybe even sickness, unforgiveness, or anger over a loss?

Have you unknowingly agreed with the enemy that these words, these circumstances, are who you are? Have you started to believe that it's just the way it is, the luck of the draw? Have you made an agreement that needs to be broken?

I don't know what's on your wall; I'm not sure if you have one. I'm not sure if your wall is short or tall, thin or thick, covered with an array of words, or holds just one. Regardless, if you have a wall, I have some good news for you.

Jeremiah 29:11(NIV) says,
"For I know the plans I have for you," declares the Lord, "plans to prosper you and not to harm you, plans to give you a hope and a future."

GOD HAS A HOPE AND A FUTURE FOR YOU; THE DEVIL WANTS YOU STUCK IN DEFEAT.

Let me get this off my chest. God did not create that wall standing between you and all He has for you. God did not paint the dark, heavy, deafening words of death on your wall either. The Devil did. God has a hope and a future for you; the devil wants you stuck in defeat. He and his agents have been hard at work trying to keep you from the greatness God has for you. The enemy would love nothing more than for you to deny God's greatness and keep you from knowing that your Creator would have anything great for you. But remember, God wants to prosper you; He has great things for you. The enemy wants nothing more than for you to blame, argue, and be mad at God for all the darkness and dread that has found its way onto your wall. Satan wants you to think that God's greatness is a joke, that it's a façade, untouchable, untrue, and unrealistic. He wants to blind you from your worthiness and from God's truth. He will go all out to accomplish this mission. He will use anyone or anything. He hates when you see yourself as you truly are, a child of the Most High God. Capable, equipped, called, and ready.

In order to break down any wall that could be standing between you and your gifts, one of the first things you need to understand is that there is an enemy and he is out to take you down. He knows the authority you have been given from God, so he will do all that he can to keep you from knowing and using that yourself. You have authority over the enemy. You have the weapons to fight him off and keep him under your feet. You have the power to shatter your wall, and you have the privilege as a child of the King to help yourself to your gifts, your spread, your banquet table.

Ephesians 2:8,10 (NLT) says,
"God saved you by His grace when you believed. And you can't take credit for this; it's a gift from God. For we are God's masterpiece. He has created us anew in Christ Jesus, so we can do the good things he planned for us long ago."

> YOU HAVE THE POWER TO SHATTER YOUR WALL, AND YOU HAVE THE PRIVILEGE AS A CHILD OF THE KING TO HELP YOURSELF TO YOUR GIFTS, YOUR SPREAD, YOUR BANQUET TABLE.

If you hear nothing else, know that God has a plan for you, a purpose for you and for your future. He loves you in the most outrageous, audacious way possible. He has the most lavish spread of greatness sitting, waiting, prepared just for you.

I'm telling you right now, what we read in Ephesians 3:20 is absolutely true: He is able to do exceedingly and abundantly more; beyond anything we could ever think, dream, or imagine.

It is no joke. He is for real; God is not messing with us. He already has everything ready. He knows exactly what we need and when we need it. As a matter of fact, I believe we have access to all of it right now; we just have to figure out how to get it. Maybe, like me, there has been a wall in your way, or as I mentioned above, maybe you have no wall at all, you've just been too distracted to notice your gifts. Or is it possible that some of us see the beauty He has prepared for us, yet we walk around defeated, thinking we can't possibly deserve it?

If any of those circumstances are true in your life right now, this book is for you.

We're going to dig a little deeper into breaking walls down because no barrier is going to keep you from becoming all you were created to be. Not only are we going to deal with breaking that wall down, but we need to understand how to keep that wall down. Being prepared and ready is vital. We need to know how it got there in the first place and what our hope and faith have to do with walking in our gifting. Understanding who you are is ridiculously important and understanding the heart of our Father is even more so. All hell will break loose trying to keep you from knowing and applying God's truth, but that's okay. Just one of those gifts will be worth the fight.

I've been there. I've seen the banquet table beautifully prepared. I've seen the wall, and I've shattered that sucker. I've stepped up to my table, unwrapped, and experienced some of the most amazing, outrageous gifts you can imagine. You can, too!

Let's jump into this thing together and start shattering some glass, my friends.

2

Yup, I Yelled at God

THEN CHECKED TO SEE IF ANYONE HEARD

I'll never forget the first time I met my husband's little brothers. They were the cutest little things. If I recall, they were eight and nine, completely adorable and full of energy. Meeting them was really special for me because I knew I was going to marry their big brother. Yes, it's true, I knew I was going to marry the man of my dreams after our first date. When I met them, I thought, awe, one day, these are gonna be my little brothers, too. I was so excited, and that's when it happened. They called me by my husband's ex-girlfriend's name. Umm, excuse me?!?!

I was calm, collected, and kind. As a matter of fact, I think my husband, boyfriend at the time, was way more uncomfortable than I was. But I said, "Oh no, you've got the wrong girl."

I immediately proceeded to let them know who I was, and I wanted to be sure they saw me for me. I wanted them to know without a doubt that the old has gone and the new has come. I mean, come on somebody, do you feel my pain here?

I'm laughing as I'm typing this because it's true. I did not want to be known as someone I was not. I was not that ex-girlfriend. I was Dianne, and I wanted them to know that. I wanted them to know me.

Have you ever had a case of mistaken identity in your life? Has someone ever labeled you or assumed you to be something or someone you're not? If so, then you know exactly what I'm talking about.

I can't help but wonder if I've ever hurt the heart of God because I didn't know the real Him. I mean, look at Jesus; He is the ultimate example of mistaken identity. He walked the earth fully man, yet fully God, and so many didn't see Him for who He was.

I have this vivid memory about a time when I yelled at God, and after realizing what I did, I was kind of scared. I mean, I know who God is, and I should have never yelled at him. Luckily, He knows me and my heart, and He loved me through it. Looking back, I was so wrong. The truth is, I didn't understand the heart of my Father. I had mistaken Him for someone He was not. Let me explain.

SAY WHAT?

It was a normal Sunday morning. We did what we always do and still do; we scooped the kids up, loaded them in the car, and made our way to church. I can remember this particular Sunday so clearly. What I used to label as one of the worst days of my life, I've come to rename as one of the best.

Our pastor at the time was doing a great job bringing God's Word to life; the story being taught was one that used to always baffle me. It was about Abraham and Isaac. You can find it in Genesis chapter 22 if you want to stop and quickly read it. Either way, I'll summarize.

Although this scripture has always caught my attention, this particular Sunday, God had something specific to work out in me. Little did I know, it would take the following seven years for me to fully understand.

As a child who grew up in church, I remembered hearing the story of Abraham and how God told him to take his son up on the mountain, build an altar, and place his son on that altar and sacrifice him. I just always remember thinking, *What?!?!* Typically, I would just blow it off and think nothing more of it knowing the outcome was a good one.

But in all honesty, I've been a bit baffled by it. I mean, who gets a promise from God to be the father of all nations, yet doesn't have a son? Then, when he finally gets his son, he's 100 years old, and God says, "Um, Abraham? I'd like you to take your son that you waited, like, 35 years for, the son that's going to make my promise for your life come true... you know, the one that's going to make you the father of all nations? I'd like for you to take him to the top of the mountain, build an altar, and then tie him to that altar, and sacrifice him."

Excuse me... what?

I cannot be the only one who thinks this is a ludicrous request.

As many times as I've been baffled by it in the past, this particular Sunday was no different. As I sat there in the pew next to my husband, I found myself becoming frustrated, and the frustration quickly turned into anger. Then, I heard what I know now was the Spirit of God whisper, "Would you do that for me?" *Wait, hold on. This makes for a great Bible story, but if you're going to get all real-life on me here God, then I guess you leave me no choice but to get all real-life right back.*

I literally said, "God, I would never do that for you." I mean, I have two beautiful children, and they are the loves of my life.

There it was. I had officially done something I hoped I would never do. I said no to God. I felt torn and sad because I longed to honor Him in every way. I was the biggest cheerleader there was for Him and His work, but angry at the same time because He had asked me this. No, I wouldn't; I couldn't. I was just being real. I said to God, "I would never tie my kids to an altar and sacrifice them for you. As a matter of fact, I can't even believe that a loving God, the Creator of us all, would ever even ask such a thing." You see, I couldn't give Him everything, simply because I did not know or understand the true nature of who He was, who He is.

YOU SEE, I COULDNT GIVE HIM EVERYTHING, SIMPLY BECAUSE I DID NOT KNOW OR UNDERSTAND THE TRUE NATURE OF WHO HE WAS, WHO HE IS.

I was so caught up in His question that I couldn't see what He was doing. I didn't realize that when He spoke to Abraham, God never intended for Isaac to be hurt. He just wanted to know the depth of Abraham's heart.

Mine, unfortunately, was not in the same place as Abraham's.

Although I knew God's request turned out to have a beautiful ending, I was so frustrated, so angered by the question that I couldn't make my way to the outcome. I couldn't see the outcome for me. I had blinders on, and I became guarded and angry.

You may be thinking, *Relax Dianne, God really wasn't expecting you to sacrifice your children.*

My response to that: "Yes, He was." I know not literally, obviously; that would be wrong. What I've learned is that God wanted and needed to know that nothing, not even my own children, was more important to me than Him. At that moment, I could not say that, not in the way He was asking.

Because of His audacious request, I began to question God in a way I never had before, and God chose to show Himself to me in a way He never had before.

His question brought me to my knees more times than I can count. It opened a door for me to experience Him in a way I never knew was possible. His inquiry brought me to a place where my comfort began to make me uncomfortable. You see, He will never make us do anything, but He's likely to give you an opportunity you wouldn't dare pass up. For me, He brought me before two doors. One door would allow me to love Him and live the rest of my life loving Him and believing in Him but doing so from behind my wall. But the second door, oh the beauty of the second door. That's the door which would allow me to experience Him as He had always intended. A place where the wall would be shattered, and I could take the gifts He had prepared just for me.

WHEN IN THE STALL... WRESTLE (OR CRY)!

Little did I know, the moment that I became real with God, the moment I told Him no, turned out to be the exact moment that the bottoms of my running shoes hit the blacktop. I'm not proposing that every "no" turns into a "yes" with God. Thankfully, mine did, but I believe it was because my heart really did believe in the greatness of God; I just didn't fully understand Him. I still don't. I'm not sure that I ever will (I mean He is God, who could ever understand Him fully?) But I'd like to think I know Him better now than I used to.

My heart longed for a real, honest answer; I wanted to know why He would even ask such a thing.

> HIS INQUIRY BROUGHT ME TO A PLACE WHERE MY COMFORT BEGAN TO MAKE ME UNCOMFORTABLE.

What I didn't tell you is that as soon as I told God no, I left the service, made my way into the women's bathroom, locked myself in a stall, and cried until just about everyone had left the church. (You'll soon find that I have a thing with crying in bathroom stalls.) I wrestled with God at that moment. I told Him my heart and questioned why He would ask such a thing. Yes, I did yell at God, then peeked under the stall wall to see if anyone could have possibly heard my moment of craziness, my breakdown, my wrestling match with the Creator of the heavens and earth. Luckily, I was solo, so I continued my conversation, but now with a much softer, somber tone. I told Him that I loved Him and wanted to do whatever He wanted me to, but that request was unthinkable. All I could imagine was Abraham actually going through the motions of preparing his son for the sacrifice. It was disturbing to me. I was confused, and the Enemy was trying to take full advantage of that. But I kept my eyes fixed on the Author and Finisher of my faith. My "no" was that of a tender-hearted daughter, simply not understanding the request of her Father. It wasn't a heart jaded with the presumption of evil, just a heart that wanted to understand its Creator. A heart that longed to experience Him, and because of that, I believe God used my "no" to set me up for the "yes" of a lifetime.

AM I RECOMMENDING THAT YOU YELL AT GOD? ABSOLUTELY NOT! AM I ADVOCATING THAT YOU TELL GOD "NO"? ABSOLUTELY, POSITIVELY NOT! AS A MATTER OF FACT, PLEASE DONT. WHAT I AM ASKING YOU TO DO IS TO BE REAL WITH HIM. HE ALREADY KNOWS YOUR HEART; HE JUST WANTS YOU TO WILLINGLY SHARE IT WITH HIM.

Am I recommending that you yell at God? Absolutely not! Am I advocating that you tell God "no"? Absolutely, positively not! As a matter of fact, please don't. What I am asking you to do is to be real with Him. He already knows your heart; He just wants you to willingly share it with Him.

I believe one of the greatest victories we can ever achieve is getting to the point where we can proudly and authentically be who we were created to be, flaws and all. To live like this, in true freedom, we must first be willing to dig deep to get to the bottom of things. We've got to be able to work through our past and present issues, hurts, pains, or whatever it is that's keeping us from moving into the best "yes" of our lives; a yes to God.

If you're struggling in your faith, why is that? If you're questioning God's sovereignty, why? If you don't understand why bad things happen, it's okay to ask. It's not wrong to ask God questions. If you've ever hung around a two-year-old for any amount of time one thing is evident, they ask questions, a lot of questions. It's okay to feel like a toddler in our faith, asking God why over and over again. It's how we learn.

Our faith is a journey. Just like growing from a child to an adult, we grow in our spiritual life. Be real with God; ask Him questions. I don't suggest yelling at Him like I did, but be real; He knows it all anyway. Talk to Him like He's your Daddy because truth be told, He is. He carries every attribute of the perfect Father.

He is constant and true. He's faithful, strong, stable, and never failing. He's bold, courageous, and all-knowing. He's the beginning and the end, the Alpha and the Omega. He's love, literally; it's the very core of who He is. He is full of grace and mercy. His love knows no ends. He's our comforter and shelter, our rock and our refuge. He's our protector and healer. He's giving and encouraging. He's patient and kind, tender-hearted, and compassionate. He's full of favor and blessing. He's giver and taker, maker of every good and perfect gift. He's everything we need and more, always walking with us and guiding us. He's leading us, directing our steps, and making our paths straight.

YOU SEE, GOD ALWAYS LOVES US RIGHT WHERE WE ARE, BUT THANKFULLY, HE LOVES US WAY TOO MUCH TO LET US STAY THERE.

One of the first steps we need to take, in receiving all God has for us, (remember those beautifully wrapped gifts?) is to get to know the Gift Giver. We need to know His heart, in order to be willing to go on this journey with Him. We will break through the walls of shame and lies as we learn how God really sees us and get to know Him better. You see, God always loves us right where we are, but thankfully, He loves us way too much to let us stay there.

3

Unmerited Favor

YOU TOOK MY WHAT?

I was crazy blessed to grow up in the church. I love the church. What a privilege it was for me to grow up learning about Jesus and all He did. I remember the series and the songs, Vacation Bible School and Sunday school, the teachers who truly desired for all of us kids to understand God's love for us. I remember learning so much from them as a child.

It wasn't long after meeting my husband that I found myself completely shocked at the fact that he didn't grow up with the privilege I had. He had never heard about Noah and the Ark and Moses and the Ten Commandments. I mean, he had heard of them, but he was in awe at the thought of all those Bible stories and characters actually being real life. He was shocked. I remember thinking, what's the big deal? Looking back, I realized I had lost my wonder. I had lost the awe in who God was. To me, those stories were normal, but if I were to investigate my

> I WAS BLINDED. I WAS A BELIEVER, BUT THE TRUTH HAD NOT FULLY SET ME FREE YET.

beliefs, then I'd have come to the conclusion that my faith wasn't all that personal. I believed in God and His son, Jesus. I believed the stories in the Bible; I believed that Jesus died and rose again, but if you had asked me if God would do any of that "Bible stuff" in the here and now, that He would come through miraculously for me now, I would have said no. I believed all of it for everyone else, but I struggled deeply believing it for me.

The Enemy is so sneaky and quite genius when it comes to distracting us from the truth. Hopefully, some of you can relate to his devious strategies. Actually, my heart's cry is that you can't, but I have a feeling most of you will.

I mentioned how God has worked some miracles in my life over the past decade, and one of my favorites is what I like to call my "revelation of righteousness."

LISTEN TO ME FRIENDS; THE DEVIL WILL DO ALL HE CAN TO TRY AND COVER YOU IN CONDEMNATION. HE LONGS TO KEEP YOU BOUND AND TIED TO THAT HELLISH PAST, BECAUSE IF HE CAN, YOU WILL NEVER FIND FREEDOM. YOU WILL NEVER BECOME ALL YOU ARE CREATED TO BE. YOU'LL NEVER EXPERIENCE THE TRUE GIFT OF THE CROSS.

One of the lies the enemy used in my life as a new believer was thinking I couldn't understand the Bible on my own. For instance, I mentioned I grew up in church, but up until a handful of years ago, I never fully understood what righteousness was. I knew John 3:16 (NIV), "For God so loved the World that he gave his one and only Son, that whoever believes in him shall not perish but have eternal life."

I knew I was saved, but something was missing. Through all those years, I somehow never grasped the truth that is necessary for a believer in Christ. I never understood what Jesus actually did for me, Dianne Wyper, on that old rugged cross I frequently sang about. I was blinded. I was a believer, but the truth had not fully set me free… yet.

Yes, I was free, saved from the depths of Hell, but I wasn't completely free because I didn't realize the fullness and the beauty of the gift I had accepted—the gift of Jesus, the gift of salvation. For years, I loved, I served, I prayed, I grew, and I did all I knew to do, but I still had constant conversation with God about His truth, His promise sounding a bit too good to be true. Surely there would be some condemnation in Heaven for my sin. Surely, it's not simply forgiven. Surely there is a price I have to pay. I would ask for forgiveness daily for the same sins. I would find myself worrying about how God was going to punish me. I had a hard time grasping the fact that all I read about was true, possible, and available for me. I was stuck.

The crazy thing is I truly believed it for everyone else. I knew God loved them and had forgiven them, but me, well, that was a different story because I knew my past. I really thought there would be a price to be paid on my part. Listen to me friends; the Devil will do all he can to try and cover you in condemnation. He longs to keep you bound and tied to that hellish past, because if he can, you will never find freedom. You will never become all you are created to be. You'll never experience the true gift of the cross.

So, yet again, another set of blinders fell to the ground, I experienced another moment in time that would forever change my thinking. It was a moment that molded my heart and retrained my brain. It was another beautiful conversation with my Jesus.

This time, I was sitting at my dining room table reading. The book was *Destined to Reign* by Pastor Joseph Prince. As I began to read intently through this beautiful book of wisdom, I stumbled upon a story of a man who used God's truth, His spoken word, to overcome some of the Enemy's work in his life. The concept was quite simple. He began to speak God's truth over and over, day after day, moment after moment.

Here's what challenged me: the specific truth that this man was claiming day in and day out over his life. It wasn't a method I had been using, and honestly, I didn't really get it, but the testimony was a powerful one, so I decided that I was going to try it.
The phrase he spoke over and over was taken from 2 Corinthians 5:21 (NIV),

"God made him who had no sin to be sin for us, so that in him we might become the righteousness of God."

The phrase that captured my attention was this: I am the "righteousness of God" through Christ Jesus.

I quickly claimed that phrase, that truth, that scripture.

I was like, "Okay, I can do this." Right then and there, sitting at my dining room table, I began to speak this truth out loud over and over. After about the tenth time, I remember becoming so frustrated and irrationally irritated.

Why? Because I realized as I was speaking this truth over and over, but I really had no idea what it meant.

In the midst of all that frustration, I just blurted out, "God, what does this mean? What does it mean that I am the righteousness of You through Your Son? I don't get it!"

And then, breakthrough! I heard the words whispered in my spirit, "Dianne, I took your hell for you."

I sobbed. Seven words. Seven huge, wall-breaking words changed my life.

> SEVEN WORDS. SEVEN HUGE, WALL-BREAKING WORDS CHANGED MY LIFE.

Please, no theological debating here. I'm not saying Jesus actually went to hell. I haven't found a scripture that says that. There are assumptions and debates, but that's not why I'm sharing this. I'm saying what He whispered to me that day is what brought absolute clarity. He took what I deserved.

When I heard Him whisper, my heart broke into two. I've read before that Jesus took my sin, but in that instant, it was like all the layers of uncertainty had been removed, and my wall of unbelief had been shattered. For the first time in my life, I understood the gift of salvation, unmerited favor, for what it truly was.

The best part of all, I understood it was done for me. Jesus did it for me. He paid the unthinkable price, the most horrific death, so I could be saved from my own sins. He took my punishment. He bore my shame.

Jesus paid the price I deserved. He paid the price you deserve, the price we all deserve for our sin. I made the choice to sin, to hurt, to steal, and to lie. I was not a nice person at one point in my life.

> I AM THE RIGHTEOUSNESS OF GOD THROUGH CHRIST JESUS. THIS MEANS WHEN GOD THE FATHER LOOKS AT ME, HE SEES ME PURE, JUST LIKE HIS SON.

My past haunted me, but no more.

I finally understood it. I finally believed it.

I am the righteousness of God through Christ Jesus. This means when God the Father looks at me, He sees me pure, just like His Son. I am now righteous (which means right with God by the way), because of what Jesus did. He views the work of His Son, Jesus, covering me. He does not see my sin, my shame, my past, but a child, His child, cleansed and purified through the work of the cross, through the sacrifice of His Son. This is grace. This is unmerited favor.

Jesus took my punishment, and He took yours as well. You don't have to carry it. You simply have to accept Jesus to experience His true freedom. He loves you; don't let the Enemy deceive

you. If you don't understand something in the Bible, ask God to reveal it to you. Ask Him to give you insight and knowledge, wisdom, and understanding. He wants to tell us, but He respects us enough to wait until we ask.

We receive not because we ask not.

Whoever asks for wisdom, wisdom will be given.

Seriously friends, this was such a life-changing revelation for me.

IT'S ALREADY BEEN DONE

Maybe you're reading this and saying, "I get it, I understand the whole righteousness thing. This is Bible 101 stuff." Then I say to you, awesome! Share it, teach it, speak it, let the world know; help them truly understand this precious gift. Too many of us have been blinded for way too long. Too many of our brothers and sisters are living with a wall of unworthiness and unbelief standing between them and all God has for them. Not because they want to, but because they just don't see it.

When I first walked into that banquet room, all I could see were the gifts. The wall was there, but I didn't see it. I wasn't stopped by it until I tried to take what belonged to me. So often, believers get overwhelmed and frustrated because they aren't able to reach the gifts, whether those be answered prayers, restored relationships, financial provision, whatever. So often we look at our lives and say, "Well God, if you are who You say You are and can do what You say You can do, then why is my prayer not getting answered? Why is my situation still the same? Why am I still sick? Why am I always broke? Why am I always feeling overwhelmed?" Listen to me; God's already provided the answer. It's sitting on the table before you, waiting for you to take, but there is another one at work in our lives, one doing all he can to defeat, distract, and destroy; One who wants nothing more than for you to think that those gifts are untouchable. Why do you think the glass was clear? Satan could care less that I could see my gifts; he just didn't want me to be able to touch them because then who would I blame? I would have blamed God, that is until God allowed me to see my wall for what it truly was, one filled with the lies, distractions, and defeat of the enemy.

As children of God, we must understand that everything we need has already been provided through the victory of the cross. The Enemy knows this and is violently angered by it. He's terrified you just might figure it out for yourself. He will lie, cheat, and deceive you in any way that he can, making you think God's not answering you when in reality, the gift, the answer has already been made available. It's sitting, waiting.

> AS CHILDREN OF GOD, WE MUST UNDERSTAND THAT EVERYTHING WE NEED HAS ALREADY BEEN PROVIDED THROUGH THE VICTORY OF THE CROSS.

Let's go back to the beginning. When Adam sinned in the Garden of Eden and ate from the tree of the knowledge of good and evil, he handed his authority over to the Enemy, the authority which was given to him from God in Genesis 1:26-28. Adam had been given authority over every living thing in and on the earth. It was for him to control. When Adam was approached by the Serpent, he was supposed to take authority over him, but he didn't. He willingly handed his authority over.

One interesting revelation that I've learned over the years is that the Devil is a spiritual being, meaning he has to have a body to work through. We have to give him the ability to work in us. Without our willingness, he can't accomplish his will through us. Fast forward, Jesus came with the mission of getting the keys of authority, of dominion back for man. He came to earth as a man (yet fully God), and He conquered. He accomplished His mission. He took the keys back from the Devil, the keys that Adam willingly handed over. Now, we have access to that authority once again through Jesus. The Devil can try to deceive us all he wants, but because of Jesus, because of the cross, he cannot defeat us unless we allow him to. Through Christ, we are the victors, not the enemy! If you hit a wall every time you try to take what God offers you, ask God to pour out a revelation of righteousness on you. Ask Him to show you who you truly are and what has already been done for you. Ask him to reveal your wall so you can know exactly what you need to do to get it down.

We must understand all Jesus has done for us. Our identity needs to rest in the fact that we are children of the King and believe no wall can stand in our way. We must confidently accept the fact that we have full rights and access to our table, and we are the righteousness of God through Jesus. It's the most beautiful revelation you will ever have the privilege of understanding.

So, if you've received righteousness, if you've unwrapped that gift, help others find their box, and cheer them on as they rip it open. Speak truth and be a wall-breaker for those around you. Honestly, so many don't see themselves for who they truly are: pure, blameless, righteous, and worthy.

It took having a come to Jesus "again" moment at my dining room table for me to finally understand grace, unmerited favor, truth, and what the gift of salvation really is. I now knew how God saw me, but what came next was grasping the importance of how I saw myself.

> OUR IDENTITY NEEDS TO REST IN THE FACT THAT WE ARE CHILDREN OF THE KING AND BELIEVE NO WALL CAN STAND IN OUR WAY.

4

Sickness, Debt, and Notecards

DEFEAT TO VICTORY, THE DOLLAR STORE, AND JESUS

It all started the Sunday morning that I said no to God. Remember the wrestling match I had with Him in the bathroom stall? That moment, that "no." This was the night that my spiritual awakening began. What I started to experience was hard to put into words. I had never felt anything like it before.

It was as if my thoughts were not my own anymore. Out of nowhere, I became covered in a blanket of fear. Every irrational thought you could imagine raced through my mind so fast, one after another, that I couldn't catch them if I tried. I was blindsided. I had no idea what I was experiencing or where it had come from. I tried everything I could think of to change these thoughts and worries, to stop them or control them, but no matter what I did, they would not cease.

They covered me, weighed me down, and tripped me up. Moment by moment, day by day, the blanket of anxiety became heavier and heavier. I was suffocating.

Being the insecure person I was, I didn't tell anyone because I thought they would think I was crazy. I mean, this can't be normal. These thoughts can't be normal; no one should be scared and overwhelmed by everything all the time.

It was absolutely exhausting. Being weighed down and anxious every second of every day, yet doing all that I could to try and remain in a normal state of mind when people were around me was draining.

WHAT STARTED OUT AS FRUSTRATED ANGER TOWARD GOD MORPHED INTO A DEEP AND DESPERATE CRY FOR HIM TO RESCUE ME AND SAVE ME.

I was so confused and angry. At first, I began to blame God. I was mad at Him. *Just because I was real with you in the bathroom stall, you're gonna leave me? You're gonna give up on me?*

There were many moments when I questioned Him like that, so many instances I would doubt His love and purpose for me. Yet, all along, He knew what He was doing. What started out as frustrated anger toward God morphed into a deep and desperate cry for Him to rescue me and save me.

It's amazing how when we become desperate for Him, we suddenly find time to consume every minute of our day crying out to Him, and that's exactly what I did. Day after day, I would cry out to Him, and day after day, I got nothing. Yet, somehow, deep in my heart, I knew He was there. I just knew it. I believed His Word, and I knew He wouldn't ever leave me.

I held tight to the words Moses spoke over Joshua in Deuteronomy 31:8 (ESV),

"It is the LORD who goes before you. He will be with you; He will not leave you or forsake you. Do not fear or be dismayed."

I knew God was with me, and He would never leave me. I trusted Him with that. Even when I didn't feel it, I always believed it. Even with no recognizable response, I kept crying out, knowing He was there and hoping He would respond.

After a few months, I still had no relief. I finally told my husband I thought I was going crazy and asked him to pray over me. Of course, he did, and his prayers brought peace momentarily, but the peace never seemed to last. We also talked to our pastor at the time, and he prayed over me and encouraged me with the Word.

I did not see a doctor. Right or wrong, I just didn't. If you're struggling and feel like you should, then by all means do. I prayed about it daily, and I knew it was a spiritual attack.

I was confused as to why my prayers were not being answered. I didn't get it. Why wasn't this breaking? I finally remember saying to God, "I can't handle this. I'm not sure what you're doing, but I can't handle this."

I blamed God for my hellish experience as if He was the one hitting me with it. He wasn't the one hurting me. The Devil was.

For some reason, we tend to hurt and blame the ones we love most when we are hurting. Is that not a truth bomb right there? I loved God, but I was hurt, so I was taking it out on Him. I figured if God loved me, He would snap His fingers and take all my pain away. After all, that's what I would do if I were Him. Clearly, I'm not God, and I am grateful for His sovereignty over my life. I'm thankful for His ability to comprehend what my mind could never fathom.

> I BLAMED GOD FOR MY HELLISH EXPERIENCE AS IF HE WAS THE ONE HITTING ME WITH IT. HE WASN'T THE ONE HURTING ME. THE DEVIL WAS.

You see, God was with me. He knew exactly what I could and could not handle, and He was there by my side every step of the way. He had His hand on my life, and He was protecting me. He wouldn't let the Devil push harder than I could withstand. I believe God was just waiting for me. He already provided my answer through the cross, but I believe He was simply waiting for me to make a choice, to take a stand, to choose Him above all else.

After telling my husband and my pastor and doing tons of research on my own about my newfound anxious state of mind, I decided to take measures into my own hands and attempt something new. I tried everything. I found myself staying up all hours of the night reading scripture, constantly crying out to God. I found myself writing, crying, sobbing, and fasting, but I wasn't exercising. I had this brilliant thought to get my endorphins pumping by working out. Everything I read said that getting your endorphins going would make you feel better. This seriously was my plan, and it's exactly what I did. Desperate circumstances call for desperate measures, and I was absolutely desperate. If God wasn't going to answer, I was going to find someone who would. My choice for the moment was—yup, you guessed it—Billy Blanks. Oh yeah, Tae Bo baby. It was going to wash all my fears away. I'm dead serious; I put my hope in Tae Bo. Surely, Tae Bo and Billy would not fail me. Working out was going to fix this mess that I had found myself in.

I put the tape in my VHS player (for the love, that makes me sound so old), put my workout clothes on, and grabbed my bottle of water. I hit play and began the workout of a lifetime. I was giving it my all, pushing through the pain, sweating, crying, yelling, screaming, kicking, and then, I broke. I broke hard. Between the squats and the karate kicks, I had a complete meltdown. I had hit an absolute breaking point.

I ran into my bedroom, fell back on my bed face up, and fully surrendered, and I simply said, "What do You want? What is it? You can have it. Whatever You want, you can have it. I'm done being my own; I'm Yours, all of me, everything."

And then I said the following, out loud, full of passion, and completely willing, "I'll even go to Africa for you!"

That sounds funny now, but it was a true cry of my heart. My whole life, even as a little girl, I remember saying to God, "Please don't make me leave my family and go to Africa." I was always terrified He would call me to leave my family. I must have grown up seeing one too many missionary videos.

Whatever I was holding onto, I let go and told God I would go to Africa. I can only imagine the chuckle that must have stirred up in his heart.

Africa! What? I'm sure He was grateful for my willingness, but looking back, Africa was never what God was asking of me.

In that moment, I was just being real. I had no idea what He wanted; all I knew was that I was willing to give Him anything, even if that meant packing up and moving to a faraway land. I didn't want one more second of my life to go by without Him in complete control. I didn't understand what was happening or why, but I knew He was God and my only hope was in Him. Sprawled out on my bed, sweaty and sobbing, I surrendered my kids, my husband, our home, my marriage, my future, and my whole life. All of it! I gave it all to Him.

SWEATY AND SOBBING, I SURRENDERED MY KIDS, MY HUSBAND, OUR HOME, MY MARRIAGE, MY FUTURE, AND MY WHOLE LIFE. ALL OF IT! I GAVE IT ALL TO HIM.

As I lay there crying on my bed, the most beautiful thing happened. The Spirit of God came upon me and covered me. The peace of God fell on me. The perfection of it was indescribable. As soon as that peace surrounded me, I heard Him speak. This was a first for me, and it was the most amazing experience I had ever had at this point in my journey with Jesus. His voice may not have been audible, but it was crystal clear. I'll never forget it. He softly said, "I have something so great for you. Just don't quit."

I have clung to those words from the moment I heard them. I meditate on them. I pray them, and I speak them. Not a day has gone by that I don't think on those words or on that moment.

THE ULTIMATE EXPERIMENT

The struggles of anxiety didn't disappear after that moment, but they did begin to dissipate. Little by little, my anxiety got better and better. Day by day, the cloud of darkness would be broken by a beam of sunlight, and soon enough, that beam took over, and the darkness drifted away.

There is something so beautiful, so powerful in hope. There is something so profound in possibility.

It was the spoken word of God over my life that changed things for me. It was then that I knew there was more for me, and I wasn't going to stop until I found it.

IT WAS THE SPOKEN WORD OF GOD OVER MY LIFE THAT CHANGED THINGS FOR ME.

If you happen to feel or know the pain of that lingering cloud of darkness, can I just speak life over you right now? There is hope! God says it. He may not have spoken it to you the same way He spoke to me, but His words are truth both for me and for you.

He says in Jeremiah 29:11a (ESV), "For I know the plans I have for you." That's not a lie; the Devil may be trying to push you around, but God knows the plan. What the Devil means to use to defeat you, God will turn around for your good and His glory.

Are you hearing that today? What is it that the Enemy is throwing your way to try to take you out? If he's after you, it's because he's scared of you.

That's exciting! Let that fire you up; let that stir in your heart for a little bit. If he's pressing you, it's because you have something in you he's afraid will come out. Be inspired by that. Be courageous and take a stand.

I didn't realize it in the moment, but those nights when I stayed awake, searching, studying, reading, and those endless cries to God and pleas with Him to hear me, they were heard. God is faithful, and He brought wisdom, understanding, and hope. This is exactly what stirred up a passion in me to take on the Devil as I lay sick, yet again, years later, this time, in a hospital bed.

I had been down this road of sickness before, but this time it had gotten worse. This wasn't the first round of testing and probing, bloodwork and appointments all in the hopes of trying to figure out what was wrong with me. I lay there with a body that was failing and not one logical answer as to why. The doctors began to wonder if I was depressed. Anxious a few years prior, yes, but at this point, I had been at least three years free from anxiety. I was not depressed. Frustrated but not depressed. Upset and annoyed but not depressed. I was a joyful person, just sick.

I CAN'T SAY I DOUBTED GOD'S ABILITY, BUT RATHER MY BELIEF.

I was sick and scared. I couldn't understand how God was going to use all of this. Even more so, I began to question if He would.

Imagine if your car had a large leak in its gas tank. Time and time again, you fill it up only to find that after just a few miles, you're on empty again. Similarly, I had been reading through the scriptures for years. I would fill my tank by pouring myself full of the Word, taking everything in that I possibly could, but then I'd lose it all through my gaping hole of unbelief.

This was nothing new for me. I knew that I struggled with receiving, or rather believing, the promises tucked throughout the pages of scripture.

Just like I shared at the beginning of this book, I could see all of the gifts. I believed they were there. I was just being held back by my wall of unbelief. I can't say I doubted God's ability, but rather my belief.

Through more prayer, more crying out to God, and more questions, I came up with another conclusion. I decided to turn my struggle into my challenge. This time it was not exercise, but an experiment, a challenge, one I think every person on the planet should choose to take.

I said, "Okay God, here I go. You say that You are the same yesterday, today, and forever, so, I'm going to take Your Word for what it is. I mean, if you did miraculous healings in the Bible, then I'm going to believe that you still can now." I can't say for sure, but I'm thinking at that moment, God must have smiled.

He was probably like, "Yes, please, do that! Do just that; take My Word for what it says."

That's exactly what I did, and I have never been the same.

NEW PATHWAYS

Let me fill you in a bit on this time in our lives. My husband had resigned from a comfortable job to start his own business. My sickness hit during our one year of no income and no insurance due to the new career choice. Multiple trips to the emergency room and multiple admittance in the hospital were beginning to add up.

> THINGS WERE ABOUT TO CHANGE, AND I WAS GOING TO SEE WHAT BELIEVING GOD'S WORD TO BE TRUE FOR ME COULD AND ACTUALLY WOULD DO.

After all the hospital stays, neurologist appointments, MRI's, blood work, and multiple other tests, no one could tell me why my limbs would suddenly fail me. There was no one answer as to why, multiple times a day, I would instantly become so weak that I couldn't stand. No one had a clue why my body would twitch uncontrollably for hours on end. Nothing! Not one idea as to what was wrong except that something was. So, there we were, broke as a joke, sick as a dog, two little kids, a home, and a whole lot of debt.

I was ready. Things were about to change, and I was going to see what believing God's Word to be true for me could and actually would do.

Let me clarify, I was not using God's Word with a "genie in a bottle" approach. What I was doing was trying my best to retrain my brain to believe it to be true for me.

I NEEDED HIS REVELATION, NOT MAN'S OPINION.

So, with the goal of learning to believe God's Word to be true for me, I wrote God's Word out on notecards and posted His truths all over my home. Then, I made it a point to speak these truths out loud every time I'd see one.

I had notecards everywhere. I was tired of being sick, and I couldn't find anywhere in the New Testament where someone asked Jesus to heal him and He said no. What did I have to lose? I wasn't doing this to test God; I was doing this to change me, my thoughts, and my belief.

My challenge was to take the Word of God and apply the promises to my life. I'm not looking for theological debates or opinions. I was keeping it simple. If I needed an answer, I went to the Word. I expected God, not man, to bring clarity. I needed His revelation, not man's opinion.

If you were to walk in my home during this season of my life, you would have seen notecards covering our walls from the front door, to the bathroom to the bedroom to the kitchen, taped to the coffee pot, and tucked inside cabinets. My favorite room of all was our office. Its main wall was covered from floor to ceiling in notecards of truth.

Everywhere I looked, I was reminded of God's promises and truths.

I am healed.

I am healthy.

I am strong.

I am courageous.

I am fearfully and wonderfully made.

I am loved.

I am worthy.

I am favored.

I am a child of the King.

I am filled with the Holy Spirit.

I am protected.

I am a light in the dark.

I am debt-free.

I am capable.

I am enough.

I am…

I was simply retraining my brain.

I've heard it said that our thoughts are like a well-traveled path. Imagine a flourishing field with one well-beaten path. If you were going to take a walk through that field, clearly you would walk on the well-beaten path, right? That's exactly what our brains do.

Sometimes, we must retrain our brains. We must create new pathways. It's not comfortable, and it takes constant effort because our brains will automatically want to go down the path it knows well. Over time, the less we travel the old and the more we trek the new, the more beaten the new path will become and the more overgrown the old path will become until the new is the norm.

GOD USED A BAD THING IN MY LIFE TO OPEN MY EYES TO THE POWER OF HIS WORD.

We must condition our brains to take God's Word seriously. We are simply putting two verses, Corinthians 10:5 and Philippians 4:8, into action, taking every thought captive and thinking on what is pure and right, noble, trustworthy, and praiseworthy.

We are simply retraining our brains and building our belief in who God is and what He says about us.

It was through sickness—something the Devil meant for destruction—that God took and used for my good and His glory. God used a bad thing in my life to open my eyes to the power of His Word.

He miraculously healed me. Every single doctor I went to had no answer, but God had one. He opened doors to a natural doctor that immediately pinpointed my issue and had me on a plan to restore my health in no time. Literally, the whole process was a complete miracle. The nudge I felt from the Lord to give this new option a try; going from barely walking to finding the exact person I needed to meet who could help me heal and get me walking and living normally again; a miracle! God works in different ways, but nonetheless, God works. Sometimes the healing is instant, and sometimes it's a process. Either way, it's healing, and I've received it.

Thank you, Lord, for loving me enough to do what you've done for me. I know I don't deserve a single ounce of it, but I fully receive it. You are just too good to me. Thank you, Lord!

SURPASSING EXPECTATIONS

I remember praying one day, and God telling me something very specific. He said, "Dianne, I want you to teach my people to expect my greatness."

I questioned, "God, who am I to expect anything from You?"

To which He responded, "Whose are you?"

I said, "I am Yours."

My Creator replied, "And who am I?"

I simply said, "You are God!"

And without missing a beat, I heard him whisper, "And is anything impossible with Me?"

With tears streaming down my face, I said, "No Lord, nothing is impossible with You. I am Yours, and here am I."

I knew that if I was going to teach anyone anything, I best learn it really well myself. I started with what I knew. Some past business training came in handy here. Many seminars and conferences later, I knew that I needed to clarify my goal, write it down, speak it, and believe I could achieve it. My thought was this, if this works so great in the secular world, imagine using it in the spiritual world, the very realm where God has given man authority of the earth and all that is in it. Imagine the possibilities. So that's what I did. I began to see it, expect it, and it didn't take long for me to begin experiencing it. I'm telling you; this is not self-help, positive affirmation, genie in a bottle stuff. But it is walking hand-in-hand with the Creator of the universe, partnering with Him to do His will and watching Him do the big things He promised in His Word that He could and would do if we would only believe!

God's truth is just that. Truth. We can experience all of it and in all its fullness. It's another gift on the table waiting to be ripped open. Learn His Word, believe what it says, and live it out.

That day, I wrote down all of our debt and all of our less-than-best circumstances. I wrote down everything, every area of my life and my family life that I wanted to expect God's greatness, and I said, "Okay, it starts with me."

Let me clarify something important, something hopefully you picked up on. The shift had nothing to do with the dollar store notecards I had covering the interior of my home, but it had everything to do with my expectations. I began to read God's Word and believe it to be true for *me*. As I would reference my list of less than best circumstances, what I started to see happen, was one-by-one God began to not merely meet my new expectations I had in the various areas of my life but He exceeded them. It wasn't long before I began experiencing all that He said was available. I have a long way to go. I'm just getting started. I have much to learn, but I can't hold in what He's taught me thus far. I want you to know that you can experience God's greatness in greater ways than you already are. I feel confident saying this because this is the exact thing that happened to me.

GOD'S TRUTH IS JUST THAT. TRUTH. WE CAN EXPERIENCE ALL OF IT AND IN ALL ITS FULLNESS.

Our financial situation was less than the best for many years. Things were tough, and money was tight. It was around this time that our church was offering a class of financial freedom. Obviously, we were a candidate, so we decided to sign up.

During the first class, the group leader had asked everyone in the room to write down their total debt excluding cars and homes. Here's the kicker: We knew the group leader quite well, so we decided to opt-out of this class exercise. I just knew they would recognize our handwriting. In reality, I was too embarrassed to let anyone let alone the group leader know the reality of our situation. We were in way over our heads. The student loans, medical bills, the gianormis IRS bill (due to a complete mess up on our taxes when draining our 401k to start our business; Yes. We drained our 401k), and every other debt we had managed to accumulate and was swallowing us whole. Literally, we felt lost in a sea of never-ending debt, and our boat was about to be capsized. We felt hopeless, overwhelmed, and truly didn't think anyone in that room would or could really, truly relate.

We walked into the second week of our financial class with a huge six-digit number written on the whiteboard. Everyone was gasping as they walked in and read what was displayed before all of our eyes. Underneath the gigantic six-digit number were the words, "Our Total Class Debt!"

If only I could describe to you the gnawing pangs that filled my stomach. I was about to burst into tears, but my sweet hubby looked at me, grabbed my hand and squeezed it with a smirk on his face that silently whispered, "No freaking way!!!" We both burst into a chuckle that caused the whole class to turn and stare. You guys, that giant six-digit class total held two major pieces of very significant information that hurled us into a loud laugh. A laugh that was secretly fighting back the lumps in our throats and the tears in our eyes (well at least I had tears. If Don didn't, he should have!). First of all, that six-digit figure written in huge, black numbers did not include our personal debt. Remember, we never submitted our notecard because we thought our friends would recognize our handwriting. And second, our personal debt was greater than the whole flipping class. Yes, our debt was more than the total classes debt combined.

Can you begin to understand what kind of situation we were in?

Mind you, we weren't buying crazy expensive things or spending frivolously. We had just had a few tough years. Life happened, and unfortunately, it cost a lot of money. Money that we did not have.

We obviously took the class very seriously after that moment. We knew we needed help and were willing to sacrifice and do whatever we had to do to get out from under the burden of debt. So, we sold stuff, minimized every payment we could, and put into action every debt annihilating move we could make. It helped, but we were still broke and honestly, couldn't really see the light at the end of the tunnel.

I can not tell you what claiming God's promises over our lives during this season did for us. Like I've said time and time again, this is not magic, positive affirmation, genie in a bottle stuff. It's simply God's truth. I wrote out truths that I found in God's Word regarding finances and posted them everywhere, along with all the other truths I was meditating on.

All I can tell you is that something very powerful takes place when you begin to speak God's Word over your life. As you begin to speak it, it takes root in your head and heart and you begin to believe it, like really truly believe it for you. It's not long after the belief settles in that you will begin to experience His greatness in whatever area you are believing Him for.

Some of the things that happened to us during this season are unexplainable. One instance, in particular, has to do with a very large hospital bill that we had been paying on for quite some time. This was a substantial bill from one of my boughts of sickness. Obviously, we didn't have this kind of cash sitting around in our bank account. One day, I called to increase our payment. We had made arrangements and were paying the bare minimum a month. I burst into tears when I heard what the lady on the other end of the phone say we had a zero balance. She didn't know why, but the balance that would have taken a lifetime for us to pay off at the rate we were paying on it was miraculously eliminated. It was gone. Zeroed out.

Literally, no way to describe what happened there, except a miracle. An absolutely amazing miracle! I'm not promising that your debt will miraculously disappear, but I am suggesting that God will work in mysterious ways.

I will say this. I believe wholeheartedly that God blesses those who are generous and those who make it a point to give their first fruits to Him. For many years in our life, tithing was very sacrificial. It was hard. It was like tithing or groceries because we literally tithed before we bought groceries for the week. Can I suggest that if this is where you are at, trust God and give what you can to Him. Ask him to lead you and guide you in this area. Remember that tithing or giving is more of a heart issue than a money issue. For us, we decided that we would be faithful in our tithing just like we were faithful in our marriage.

FOR MANY YEARS IN OUR LIFE, TITHING WAS VERY SACRIFICIAL. IT WAS HARD. IT WAS LIKE TITHING OR GROCERIES BECAUSE WE LITERALLY TITHED BEFORE WE BOUGHT GROCERIES FOR THE WEEK.

I can remember so many times when we were broke as a joke and had no food in the house. I'd be like, well, I guess we are going to have a piece of bread for dinner, and my sweet momma would show up at our door with a bag of groceries.

You guys, I'm not making this stuff up. Her timing was impeccable every single time it happened. She would randomly drop off toilet paper when we didn't have any or milk when I had run out and my littles needed a bottle. Every time it would happen, I would sob. Not only would I thank her, but I thanked the Lord. I just knew without a doubt that He had orchestrated the whole thing every single time it happened.

He is just so good. *Great!* I'm crying again just reminiscing about all of these moments that have proved His faithfulness time and time again in my life. He is just the sweetest Father ever!

I truly believe God is honored by giving Him the first of what you have. Not the leftovers but the first. He doesn't need our money. It's an act of thanksgiving for all that we have and all we have been blessed with. If we can't give to Him in our lack, what makes us think that we will give to Him in our wealth? As crazy as it sounds, it can be easier to give out of your lack than your wealth. Either way, if you haven't been one to generously give back to God, try it.

> IF WE CAN'T GIVE TO HIM IN OUR LACK, WHAT MAKES US THINK THAT WE WILL GIVE TO HIM IN OUR WEALTH?

So what did we do to help change our financial situation? Our family decided to give to God out of our first fruits, no matter what our bank account status was. We chose to believe God wanted us to experience His greatness, even in the area of finances. We stood on the promises in the Word of God (which I was constantly reminded of because they were plastered on notecards all over our house).

My husband Don and I were recently driving and talking, and I said, "Don, do you remember that day that I wrote everything down that I was going to expect God's greatness over? Remember how overwhelmed we were with life circumstances and how with our income and situation, there seemed no realistic way out? Do you know that I just looked at that list a few days ago, and do you know that every single thing on that list is completely wiped out?" In five years, everything is gone. What would have taken us more than a lifetime to eliminate by our own standards, God has eliminated.

In our finances, there's no way to explain how we are where we are, except the greatness of God. My health. No explanation except for the greatness of God. My faith, my hope, and my trust in Him, the greatness of God. I didn't deserve it, but He challenged me to expect His greatness in every one of these areas. He taught me to retrain my brain using His truth and dollar store notecards.

He has never failed me yet. We worked hard; don't get me wrong. We sacrificed things to pay stuff off; we took action in the areas that He said to take action in. We not only expected, but we did. We did whatever God told us to do. He multiplied our efforts, and we discovered that there is supernatural favor on those who believe with God all things are possible. What we did could have never brought us to where we are.

Some of you may be thinking, that's crazy! You can't just expect great things to happen because you post notecards in your home and read them every day. All I have to say to you is, you're exactly right. If you speak that, believe that, then I promise you, you will experience just that. You'll get no change. As a matter of fact, things will probably get worse. You must have hope.

You must have faith in what God says. You can read the healing stories in the Bible all day long, but if you don't believe they really happened and God is the same yesterday, today, and forever, then my guess is you won't grasp His greatness in that area. But, once you've bought into this aspect of God's character, you'll reap the rewards in even greater measure. Things aren't always good, but He will work them together for our good if we let Him.

This exact issue is where I was lost for so many years. I believed the healing stories of the Bible for those people, but I never believed that God would do that in the here and now. Why? Because I had never seen it in the here and now. That's not a knock to those around me, but it's the reality. I never had any sight to my faith, at least in the healing area. I said, "Ok God, let's do this! Grow my faith. Show me that Your Word is the truth. All of it, not just a little bit of it."

THINGS AREN'T ALWAYS GOOD, BUT HE WILL WORK THEM TOGETHER FOR OUR GOOD IF WE LET HIM.

When I was sick in my bed, sobbing because I just wanted to feel better, I would put His words into action. I would shut my eyes, reach my hand out, and visualize myself as the woman who reached out and touched the robe of Jesus. I actually did that over and over. All alone in the dark, I would reach my hand out and say out loud, "I know if I could just touch Your robe, I would be instantly healed. I know You would do that for me." Something about that built my faith. I saw myself being healed even when I hadn't experienced it. I would lay there, body twitching like crazy, and reach my arm out and whisper, "If I could just touch Your robe." I'd see my hand reaching out and touching His invisible hem, and I would lay there rejoicing in the healing I knew was coming. Call me crazy, but that's what I did. I believe it was in those moments that I was beginning to retrain my brain. The words on my notecards were coming to life in my mind. They weren't merely verbal words, but scripture was being brought to life for me. I was learning to use it in my own situations. His words, His healing, they are gifts. I decided to rip them open.

WERE GOING TO STAND BEFORE SOME GIANT MOUNTAINS. WE CAN CHOOSE TO SPEND OUR WHOLE LIFE TRYING TO CLIMB, OR WE CAN USE THE WORD OF GOD AND OUR FAITH IN HIM TO SIMPLY CONQUER.

Does this mean life will always be perfect, and we'll never have issues? Absolutely not. Look at the problems I needed to face to learn all of this. Trials will come, but I believe Mark 11:22-25 (ESV) wholeheartedly. I believe we play a huge part in drowning out those problems, those trials, those tricks of the Enemy. We must know there is a way, believe we can overcome, and then take action.

And Jesus answered them, "Have faith in God. Truly I say to you, whoever says to this mountain, 'Be taken up and thrown into the sea,' and does not doubt in his heart, but believes that what he says will come to pass, it will be done for him. Therefore I tell you, whatever you ask in prayer, believe that you have received it, and it will be yours. And whenever you stand praying, forgive, if you have anything against anyone, so that your Father also who is in heaven may forgive you your trespasses."

We're going to stand before some giant mountains. We can choose to spend our whole life trying to climb, or we can use the Word of God and our faith in Him to simply conquer. Climb or conquer. He's not a bossy God. He'll totally let you choose.

Let's look at some practical takeaways from Mark 11:22-25 and learn how to expect and experience God's greatness in your life:

1. Speak to your mountain; tell it to get out of your way.

2. Do not doubt.

3. Believe what you ask will happen.

4. Pray for big, impossible things and expect the God of the impossible to do great things.

5. Forgive everyone for everything.

Speak to your mountains, speak to your sickness, speak to your finances, speak to your relationships. Speak to whatever it is that's standing in front of you that seems impossible to conquer and tell it to get out of your way. Live out Mark 11:22-25.

Expect His greatness in your body, expect it in your finances, expect it in your marriage, expect it in your relationships. Expect it in the lives of the lost; expect it in your ministry and your work. Learning to expect His greatness in everything is a gift just waiting to be picked up and unwrapped. Open it up and live it out!

SPEAK TO YOUR MOUNTAINS, SPEAK TO YOUR SICKNESS, SPEAK TO YOUR FINANCES, SPEAK TO YOUR RELATIONSHIPS. SPEAK TO WHATEVER IT IS THAT'S STANDING IN FRONT OF YOU THAT SEEMS IMPOSSIBLE TO CONQUER AND TELL IT TO GET OUT OF YOUR WAY. LIVE OUT MARK 11:22-25.

5

Cliffs, Ladders, and Jail Cells

WHAT THE CRAP HAVE I DONE?

Do you have a non-negotiable in your daily routine? Two of mine are coffee and music. Worship music specifically; sometimes a little Kenny Chesney, but mostly worship music. Worship is one of my favorite things in the whole world. I say it's my non-negotiable in life because when I find myself going without it, things are just off. I do my best to find moments of worship daily. Not always with music, but that is my preferred way.

One day, while driving in my car, I was singing away when suddenly, I was taken back to a very specific memory. Not a fond memory necessarily, but one that God clearly wanted me to revisit.

I rarely know why He does what He does, but with each encounter, I always end up realizing how awesome He is.

He brought to my mind a time in my late teens when I went cliff diving.

Weird that this moment was brought up because there is nothing special about this adventure. As a matter of fact, as I mentioned above, I'm not fond of it. I try to forget some moments of my life because, for a long time, I was just one big hot mess.

I saw myself packed in a car with a bunch of friends, all on our way to experience what we believed to be life at its fullest. We were going on an adventure. We were making our way to a specific cliff; one we were going to jump off. I suddenly began to relive the feelings of uncertainty, fear, and pressure. I wasn't a strong swimmer at all, but when you're in your teens, sometimes the pressure of your friends encourages your brain to make a fake left in the area of logic.

Needless to say, I knew I probably shouldn't jump. When we arrived at the destination, I knew even more that I should not jump, but of course, I did anyway.

It was actually a lot of fun; I had never experienced such an adventure in my life. I felt like a daredevil and totally loved every ounce of the adrenaline rush that flooded my mind and shocked my body. My mom would have died if she knew what I was doing, but at that age, I just did it anyway. (Sorry Mom!)

As I'm replaying this memory in my mind, God brought to my attention a verse my two-year-old niece had recently learned and recited to my whole family, a verse that my family has now learned because of her stinking cuteness. That sweet little love is sharing God's love at two, and she doesn't even realize it.

The verse is this: "When my heart is overwhelmed, lead me to the rock who is higher than I." Psalm 61:2b (KJV)

At that moment, the memory made sense, and so did the message God was revealing to me.

Once I jumped off that cliff, exhilaration filled my body from head to toe. It was amazing. I dreamed of moments like that. Freedom was mine. The liberation and excitement were out of this world until I landed. The landing not only hurt, but it was at that moment, I realized I was no longer on solid ground (remember at the time, I was less than best at swimming). I began to panic a bit, and I didn't know what to do. The water was cold and rough. I struggled to keep my head above the crashing waves. My legs and arms grew tired, and I didn't realize how high of a cliff I actually jumped from until I was in the water looking back at it. All I wanted was to be back at the top of that rock.

The problem was I didn't know how to get there, how was I supposed to climb back up? There was supposed to be a ladder someone had hung to climb back up to safety, but in the midst of the raging water, I couldn't find it. I was so tired, and there was no one to help me.

Just me in a sea of cold, dark water that was crashing up against a solid, massive rock, the one from which I had willingly leapt off.

I found a small rock a little further out and made my way to it. The comfort of finding something to lean and hold onto was immensely helpful.

I stayed there for quite some time thinking, what did I just do? How did I get out here in the middle of this body of water stuck with nowhere to go?

As I'm replaying this memory in my mind, the quiet whisper of God has yet again made its way into my head and heart.

"This was you before you came back to the Rock, Me."

I began to sob. It was so intimate and personal. He knows our story better than we do.

You see, I was raised to know the Rock, to stand on the Rock, and I was reminded of what can happen to a life that chooses to take things into their own hands and leave the Rock. I was indeed the prodigal daughter. I left; I was going to figure things out on my own, so I took what I thought was the adventure of a lifetime. I moved away. I told God He was going to have to wait because I didn't really see a big difference between serving Him and not. So, I did just that. I turned away, and the adventure down that road began as fun and thrill-seeking. I loved it, but that didn't last long. I quickly found myself plummeting into the depths of those cold, dark waters. I was soon alone and tired, tired of running, tired of bad choices catching up with me, and tired of having no one I could trust.

Then, I was reminded of the Rock I once stood upon, and I began to crave that. I hungered for the peace, the security, and the love that comes with the Rock. Although it was right there, I didn't know how to get it back. There was just too much in the way. So, I found a small piece of that Rock. I changed a few behaviors, changed some friends, and began to make better choices. I was now comfortable; I was holding onto a piece of that Rock I so craved. After all, I believed John 3:16 and confessed Jesus as my Savior, but I wasn't surrendered because I was still half in the raging water and half holding onto a piece of Him, just enough of Him to make me feel okay.

The time came when I got tired of holding onto that little piece of rock. I was exhausted and cold, and I was done being tossed around by the water surrounding me. I wanted out, but the only way for me to do that was to let go of the security I had and completely let go of the things I was holding onto. I had to trust Him to get me to the fullness of all He had for me: Himself. I had to trust He would give me the strength to get from the raging water to that ladder hanging in the cleft of the cliff. I had to let go and give it all I had without turning back to that small piece of comfort. I had to push through my tired arms, my cold body, and the people yelling, distracting me from above.

I HAD TO TRUST HIM TO GET ME TO THE FULLNESS OF ALL HE HAD FOR ME: HIMSELF.

I had to follow His voice, His lead, above all else.

I made it to the ladder that day. I was scared, but I didn't let anyone know it. I climbed the ladder, which, by the way, was very unstable. Why I got talked into that adventure, I'll never know, but I made it. When I reached the top of the cliff, I stood there and thought, I am so never doing that again.

I HAD TO FOLLOW HIS VOICE, HIS LEAD, ABOVE ALL ELSE.

Of course, immediately, the pressure was on and everyone was yelling for me to jump again, but deep in my heart, I knew my answer, and I stood my ground. I stood on His ground, the Rock that is higher than I. You see, God is our solid Rock, the one safe and secure place that will never move, never change, never leave. Oh, how we need a solid foundation, a firm ground we can stand on, no matter what life throws our way. This gift, this Rock is our one constant that will never change. We can stand strong on Him, because of Him.

While driving, my sobbing lasted until I reached a parking lot (talk about giving the cars next to me something to stare at: a sobbing, singing, hot mess of a mom). I quickly pulled out my laptop and typed. Actually, these were the very words I typed that day. Sitting in a parking lot pecking away at the keys to bring these words to you, whoever you may be. The revelation that God gave me that day was a beautiful one; it brought to mind all He has done in my life, all of the crazy He has worked through on my behalf. Mostly it reminded me of His unrelenting love and faithfulness in my life. Deep down, I believe that revelation was to be shared. Maybe you're reading this, and it's you that is standing on the edge of a cliff ready to jump, following the fun leaps of those around you. Whatever your temptation may be, my plea to you is don't you dare jump! Don't leave the solid ground for a "fun little adventure" or "fresh start." Just stay put. Talk to God; ask His Spirit to guide you. The ride down may be a lot of fun, but the landing hurts, and for the love, it's a tough swim to that ladder.

THE GIFT OF A LADDER

I know not everyone who jumps off a cliff has this experience. As a matter of fact, I'm a much better swimmer now, and I can't say I wouldn't do it again someday (somewhere where it's safe).

The Spirit of God spoke this into my heart, and I want to share it. I feel too many of us are swaying back and forth in the dark cold waters, wanting to stay because it's comfortable, and by comfortable, I mean it pretty much sucks, but it's familiar and all that we know.

While being tossed around by the waves, we become intrigued by the idea of something better: choosing to let go and give our all to Jesus.

Familiarity is a lot easier, but we can't stay there forever, or we never discover the adventures He has in store for us. We'll never encounter the fullness of who He is. We'll never enter the banquet room, and we'll never experience the spread of greatness that He has specifically prepared for each one of us.

How can we climb to the peaks and journey through the valleys if we are stuck being tossed back and forth by the sea?

FAMILIARITY IS A LOT EASIER, BUT WE CAN'T STAY THERE FOREVER, OR WE NEVER DISCOVER THE ADVENTURES HE HAS IN STORE FOR US.

How can we sit on solid ground, soaking up the peace, love, and joy that only He can offer if we are stuck holding onto a slippery rock in the middle of the darkness, fighting for our security?

How can we become all that we were created to be by staying in the familiar?

We won't; we can't!

Could He reach down and grab us? Yes, He could and for some, He might. For me, it was all about the journey; it was all about the choice. I chose to jump, so I had to choose to make my way back to that rock. I had to choose to go after that ladder.

Ladders help us reach things that we could otherwise not reach. They are a blessing in disguise. For me, this ladder was a lifesaver, literally. It was a beacon of hope wrapped up in wood and rope.

This ladder served a huge purpose for me that day. It bridged a gap from one place to the next.

> HIS GREATNESS WILL TAKE YOU FROM WHERE YOU ARE TO WHERE YOU NEED TO BE.

So often in our walk with God, it's easy to feel as if we are stagnant. The illustration of being stuck out in the cold water is a great reminder of how it can feel sometimes in our spiritual journey. We can get to a point where we feel isolated, even when our faith is strong. Maybe we aren't far from Jesus in a literal sense, but somehow, we feel overwhelmed, tired, and distant.

Maybe you're struggling with a personal situation; maybe your marriage is on the verge of falling apart. Maybe the problem is on the edge of the cliff and just one more thing will push it over the side of the mountain. God has a ladder for you, a bridge of hope waiting to lead you from here to there.

His greatness will take you from where you are to where you need to be.

You don't have to jump or fall. Your financial situation doesn't have to end up in the pits. Your situation doesn't have to fail. The tough season can end. Loss doesn't have to keep you stuck. There is a way across the pit of despair; there is a way out of the trap the Enemy has set before you. Don't fall for it, and if you already have, don't you dare stay stuck there.

The ladder hanging from the side of that cliff was my hope. It's what I used to pull myself up to the solid ground. It was the hope of where I could go; what I could do.

Check this out from Hebrews 11:1 (KJV):

"Now faith is the substance of things hoped for, the evidence of things not seen."

What are you hoping for?

Restored relationships, health and healing, prosperity, purpose, financial provision? Healing for your past or victory in the present? What is it? What's your goal? What is the gift you're looking to rip open?

Are you expecting God's greatness in that area? Do you know what God's Word says about the matter? If not, go look. Write the truths out, type them up, carry them around with you, post them where you can see them, and speak them over your situation, expecting that truth to be true for you.

> GOD HAS ALREADY EQUIPPED YOU WITH WHAT YOU NEED TO GET TO WHERE YOU NEED TO GO. JUST GO DO IT.

We play such a huge role in unwrapping this precious gift of hope. Because the gift of hope is only a page away in your Bible. Psalm 119:114 (NLT) says,
"You are my refuge and shield; your word is my source of hope."

Start using God's Word and expecting His greatness, climb that ladder rung by rung until you've conquered your raging sea. God has already equipped you with what you need to get to where you need to go. Just go do it. Let go of comfort; it's a death trap. Paddle and kick, throwing one arm in front of the other and get to that ladder. Find hope, the substance of your faith. When you have something to hold onto, something to strive for, believing for it becomes a whole lot easier.

THE CELL AND A SUNDAY SCHOOL SONG

I remember my daughter as a little girl, dressing up, dancing, and singing all through the house. She was adorable. We would praise and applaud her, telling her how perfect her performance was. She would bow and curtsy, and within minutes, a new act would begin. We adored her, noticed her, and loved her, and today, we do so even more. She's amazing. She's an incredible young woman, and we couldn't be prouder of who she is.

But it proves true that girls are made with a desire to be adored, to be sought after, to be noticed and loved. Some carry those desires far beyond looking for attention as a little girl. For me, searching and seeking this attention took me many places I regret going. People hurt me, and I hurt people. Before I knew it, I began to morph into a young woman who cared only about herself and what others thought of her.

As time went on, I began to push the Jesus, who I had grown up learning about, further and further away. Well, that's what I thought at least. Looking back, He never actually went anywhere. I can remember some of the moments in my life where I was so lost, making horrible choices, and I would hear the voice of God calling me home. I would even tell people, "I don't know what I'm doing; I'm supposed to be loving and serving Jesus."

I can recall specific moments where I would say out loud, "I hope Jesus doesn't come back tonight because if He does, I will not be going home with Him."

That sounds so horrible. You're probably wondering what would possess one to say such things? It was the fact that God never left me, and I knew it. I knew He was there. He was constantly calling me, seeking me out, whispering my name, knocking on the door of my heart.

The problem was I had jumped. I couldn't find the courage to make my way back to the Rock. I was weak. I was too consumed with what everyone else thought.

But thank the Lord, the day came when I realized I could no longer keep my head above water. I needed help. I needed Jesus.

The situation is irrelevant, but the moment for me was pivotal. I was either going under or I was getting out of that raging water. If you're reading this and you have never surrendered your life to Jesus and said, "Jesus, I want to give my life to You. I just can't do it on my own anymore. I believe that You are the Son of God, that You died for my sins. I believe You rose from the dead three days later. Lord take my life, make me new, save me." If you've never done that, or if your heart is pounding, and you think you should, I invite you to stop right now and ask Jesus to be the Lord of your life.

It doesn't matter where you are or what you're going through. John 3:16 says that whoever believes can have eternal life. It doesn't say it's for those who have lived a good life and made good choices. Shoot, you don't even have to be a good person to give your life to

Jesus; I certainly wasn't, but I promise you, you will become great. He's going to flip your life upside down, and it's not with a bunch of rules and regulations. He's going to rock your world with a tidal wave of love and grace you've never experienced before, a love that you never knew existed, a love specifically for you, a love that you cannot even comprehend. Just give Him a chance; let Him in. What do you have to lose?

My pivotal, "come to Jesus" moment that I mentioned above used to be my little secret, a hidden story that no one ever knew. The secret I always kept guarded was that I gave my life to Jesus while leaning against a wall of a jail cell. I called my mom and bless her heart, she didn't even know what to say. I think she was just so disappointed that her little girl did something so stupid. But instead of condemning me, she sang. She sang to me, and the song that poured out of her lips was "Jesus Loves Me." She sang that little ol' Sunday school song to her 19-year-old daughter who was locked up in a jail cell for the night.

> WITH WHAT THE ENEMY MEANT TO DESTROY AND RUIN ME, THE LOVE OF GOD OVERCAME, ALL THROUGH A SONG I SANG AS A LITTLE GIRL.
>
> JESUS LOVES ME!

With what the Enemy meant to destroy and ruin me, the love of God overcame, all through a song I sang as a little girl.

Jesus loves me!

"Yes, Jesus loves me. Yes, Jesus loves me. Yes, Jesus loves me. The Bible tells me so."

There I was, 19, leaning against the wall of a jail cell packed full of women and my mom on the other end of the payphone singing, "Jesus Loves Me." I decided I longed for that love, and I was finally ready to say yes to Him. My way obviously wasn't working so well.

I can't say I made all the best choices after that moment, but I can say that because of that yes, God was able to begin the transformation.

At that moment in my life, my mom was my ladder; she was my bridge. She was a gift. She was the one who filled the gap between where I was and where I longed to be.

You may be that ladder for someone else. You may be the one standing in the gap for the lost child or standing for a sick family member. Maybe your faith has to be borrowed; maybe you're the hope they need to get through. Could it be there is a song in you that someone needs to hear? A soft, love-filled response against anger and frustration? Do you have a message in you, a prayer, a book, a dream, a business, a confidence, a hope, a mission, a faith so unwavering others can stand on it, believe in it, borrow it? You just might be a gift for someone else in your life.

Boldly and courageously fill the gaps, my friends. Stand strong; stand faithful. Keep your post knowing and trusting in who God is and what He has already done. Others see it; they notice. Something as simple as the words of an old childhood song became the rung on which I would cling, holding on for dear life. The words of my mother's voice became the ladder attached to the side of the cliff, providing a beacon of hope for me while being swallowed up in the crashing waves. That ladder, those words, my mother, gave me hope. You will do the same to those watching, you will feed their faith. Others will borrow it, feed on it, and grow. You may never even know it.

In my mind, I see this ladder, this bridge of hope filling the gap from one place to the next. In order to get from here to there, we have to use our faith. The hope is what gives us the sight of what can be, the hope of what's to come. The hope of healing, the hope of restoration, the hope of breakthrough.

It's by faith that we receive this hope. It's by faith that we get to the other side of the ladder, the bridge. It's by faith that we approach our banquet table and get through our wall.

> BOLDLY AND COURAGEOUSLY FILL THE GAPS, MY FRIENDS. STAND STRONG; STAND FAITHFUL. KEEP YOUR POST KNOWING AND TRUSTING IN WHO GOD IS AND WHAT HE HAS ALREADY DONE.

For God to do this, we have to learn to transfer our faith from our head to our heart. I'm willing to bet that a lot of us believe with our heads but not necessarily in our hearts. That's okay; it's part of the journey, the growth, the process.

So, how do we get things from our heads to our hearts?

We do it by speaking life into them. Matthew 12:34b (ESV) says that "…out of the abundance of the heart the mouth speaks." It's critical that we think and speak God's Word over every situation and circumstance in our lives. Our words have the power of life and death. We either speak life into things or death over things. So, to take something from our head and bring life to it, we need to breathe life into it. Our words take our faith from rung to rung, moving us across the ladder to the hope of what's to come.

Remember my vision? It was words that held my wall up, and it's through words that my wall fell. It was the spoken Word of God. Our own words don't carry enough power; they can add to our walls, but they don't carry enough weight to shatter our walls. It's the spoken Word of God that causes them to crumble. This is how we break it down.

Rung by rung, moment by moment, day by day, your words, you speaking God's truth will allow truth to find its way from your head to your heart. When you declare things, you begin to believe those things, and as you believe them, you will begin to experience them. It's not magic; it's simply God's powerful Word at work in us, His kids.

OUR WORDS HAVE THE POWER OF LIFE AND DEATH. WE EITHER SPEAK LIFE INTO THINGS OR DEATH OVER THINGS.

This is great for the one who speaks truth but sad for the one who isn't careful with their words.

Hope is a gift; words are a gift. That which we hope for, that which we think about and speak about, comes about, whether good or bad. Use the most powerful, mountain-moving words you know and speak them with confidence and faith. Speak life into your situations. I've had to learn to do it not only in my life but those placed in my life as well. I encourage you to do the same.

6

Movies and the Bathroom Stall

LEARNING WHAT IT MEANS TO BE HIS

In our house, one of our favorite traditions is family movie night. My kids go all out for these evenings. After the movie is picked, our entire home gets a complete reno. Furniture gets moved, decorations are pulled from anywhere and everywhere, and the whole house is quickly transformed into a theme which relates to the movie.

One night, instead of staying in and making the transformation in-home, we decided to go out to the local cinema. We ordered our tickets, picked our seats, and headed out for the evening.

To set things up, my son had been having a bit of a rough day. It seemed that listening to me was proving to be a little challenging on this particular afternoon. Every disrespectful word he uttered made my body temperature rise a degree. Every act of defiance was making my blood boil, and finally, I could not take it anymore. My frustration exploded, and I freaked out on my little man just before heading into the theater.

Yes, I got mad.

Have you ever had an "I'm sure everyone in this place thinks I'm a crazy out of control, mean mother," moment? Please say you can relate.

The whole situation made me so upset, I didn't even want the movie theater popcorn I'd been craving since the moment we decided to go out. In all honesty, this just made me angrier because I realized my stubbornness was getting the best of me, and because of it, I was missing out on theater popcorn (which is the *real* reason we all pay crazy amounts of money to go to the movies anyway—am I right?).

As we settled into our seats, I fumed inside. I was so worked up from the simple frustrations of a disobedient child. As I was sitting there, I tried to hold back tears that for some reason wanted to burst out of my eyeballs like a raging river pressing against a breaking, soon to be crumbled dam. I was tired. Sometimes, being a mom is hard.

Just before the tears began to swell and make their way down my cheeks, carrying a stream of black mascara and pink blush with them, this happened. My son said something that pierced my heart. If my heart could shed tears, it would have. With his head hung low and sadness painted on his face, he said, "I know I'm just a bad kid alright. I'm just bad!"

The dagger had officially been twisted. This wasn't a cry for attention, this was a real thought being released in a moment of truth. He was hurting too. He didn't want to be bad; he just had to work through the process of realizing that honoring us was expected and way less consequential than disobeying.

He felt awful; he was regretful and sad. He felt like a bad kid.

He’s not a bad kid; he's amazing. He has one of the biggest, most tender hearts. He's passionate and full of life. He's absolutely hilarious, and I know God has something extra special for Him. He's set apart; he's a world changer, but in this moment, he felt like a bad kid.

And then, you guessed it, I felt like a horrible mom because who wants their little man feeling all sad and hurt thinking he's a lousy person?

Thank goodness we aren’t expected to live based on our feelings. Can I get an amen? I mean, if that were the case, I’d be one hot mess.

Oh, how parenting can be challenging. I bit my cheeks to hold my tears back, hugged him, and reminded him that he is not a bad kid, that he is a great kid, but he must be respectful. He must obey.

I made my way to the bathroom because clearly, Momma was going to need a tissue. I was running on empty. It seemed the whole week had been this way, and this was just the last straw.

As I stood gathering tissue in the bathroom stall, the tears began to flow. I told you I have a thing with breaking down, crying, and talking to Jesus in bathroom stalls. So weird, but whatever works right?

As I tried to keep my mascara in place, I heard the Holy Spirit whisper, "So many of my kids feel that way like they're bad kids; they feel just like Braden."

Thank the Lord for sharing that wisdom with me. I get it. I've been there. I'm still there way too often. I felt like it in that moment like a failing mother. One sharp twisted emotion stabbing my heart after an already tough week. It's like the Enemy of our souls studies us and knows where to aim to inflict the most damage. He's such a loser.

> GOD IS SO GOOD. HE NEVER UNVEILS A PROBLEM OR BRINGS ONE TO OUR ATTENTION WITHOUT GIVING US A NEXT-STEP TOWARD THE SOLUTION.

God is so good. He never unveils a problem or brings one to our attention without giving us a next-step toward the solution.

Just as I tossed my mascara covered tissue in the toilet, I heard another whisper from my Creator. He said, "When it comes to helping Braden, he needs My truth about who he is spoken over him. Not condemnation, not 'Why don't you listen?' not 'You're being bad!' He needs life, truth, My Word spoken over him."

Then, He reminded me of what I needed when I was learning who I was in Christ when I had my "revelation of righteousness." I needed God's truth about who I was spoken over me daily. (Remember the notecards?)

The reality is, we all need God's truth spoken over us. It's imperative we learn to speak *that* truth over ourselves. We can't simply leave it up to everyone else. We have to know and be secure in who we are. We must know God's truth, and we have to speak it over ourselves and then over others.

That's our mission with Braden and Nevaeh, and that's my challenge to you. Knowing who we truly are in God's sight is a gift. We are the loved, powerful, righteous, holy children of Almighty God. That is HUGE!! If we don't know who we are, we can't tell others who they are. It is imperative that we learn the truth from God about who we are and who humanity is to God.

WATCH YOUR WORDS

I've learned a lot over the years about the power of our words, the power of God's spoken word. God created everything we see and, even more impressive, all that we don't see with His Words. John 1:1 (NIV) says, "In the beginning was the Word, and the Word was with God, and the Word was God." It was His faith put into words that breathed life into everything. It's absolutely amazing if you think about it. I challenge you to study this concept and ask God to give you wisdom and understanding when it comes to the power of your words.

Think about it this way: Every word you speak breathes life or death. It builds up or tears down.

You make an agreement with God or the Enemy.

> "IF EVERY WORD YOU SPOKE ACTUALLY HAPPENED, WOULD YOU CHANGE WHAT YOU SAID?"

It's true; think about it as you speak this week. Pay attention to every word you say, even if you're joking—especially then. Watch what you say. Watch what words of others you listen to and allow to be spoken over you because they, too, are speaking life or death.

One time I heard someone say, "If every word you spoke actually happened, would you change what you said?"

Wow. Think about that.

In the vision God gave me, the words on my wall, those were the things I was speaking over myself. I saw them keeping me from the things God had for me. They were not shown to me on a cute little pad of paper written with a pretty font in a bright, cheery color. They were dreadful, dark, heavy, evil. They were words of death.

I had spoken them or allowed others to speak them over me because when you speak things, you believe them.

You may not even realize this, but it happens. Your brain doesn't know whether it's good or bad, it simply walks those words down the well-beaten path, characterizing you just as you speak.

It really does not know any better. You must tell your brain what to do, and trust me, it will do it.

> GOD'S WORD CHANGES THINGS. IT BRINGS LIFE WHERE DEATH ONCE FOUND ITS HOME.

Now, remember what God told me to do to get that wall down? I had to speak His truth over it.

Just like he told me to do when I was sick, just like he told me to do with Braden.

Life-giving, faith-filled words. God's Word changes things. It brings life where death once found its home. It raises the dead and fills them with new life. It's a breath of fresh air.

Both He and His Word are life-giving!

Our words define us; they define our situations, our families, and our circumstances. Words build our faith or tear it down.

James is very clear on the impactful power of our words and the ability to tame our tongue.

You'll notice in James 3:8 he says a man can't tame it. That's precisely why we need God's truth, His words, and the Holy Spirit guiding us. We can't do it on our own.

Change your words. Let them be the weapon that shatters your wall, not the death that covers it.

By the way, don't you dare be the words on someone else's wall either.

Speak life-giving words over yourself and others. They are thought through, carefully selected, treasured gifts among those who have already received them. Proverbs 18:21 (NLT) says, "The tongue can bring death or life; those who love to talk with reap the consequences."

Begin unwrapping the truth of how much power our words hold in our lives and in those around us. When used the right way, they are yet another gift on the table of God's goodness.

CHANGE YOUR WORDS. LET THEM BE THE WEAPON THAT SHATTERS YOUR WALL, NOT THE DEATH THAT COVERS IT.

7

Being Authentically You

INSPIRATION FROM JOEL

Right now, I want you to take a look around. No matter where you are, I want you to see something. Take notice of the things completely out of your control. Find the miraculous that surrounds you.

> FIND THE MIRACULOUS THAT SURROUNDS YOU.

Whether you're snuggled up on a couch with your little loves, cooking dinner, or doing dishes, or maybe sneaking in a few pages while on a coffee break at work, look around. Discern all the miracles and blessings you encounter every day. Look at your kids (if you have them), notice their breath, their heart beating in the chest, the way their eyes dance. Step outside and notice the sun and feel the warmth of its rays. The moon is another wonder. Look at it hanging there, night after night, beautifully reflecting the light of the sun. Have you turned on a light switch or plugged something in lately? If so, then you're enjoying the beautiful gift of electricity. It's phenomenal! Are you experiencing the sounds of laughter or even the wiping off an emotional tear? Maybe you find yourself in a busy, hustling and bustling part of town. Notice the people, trains, cars, and buses; the sounds, the touch of the wind, the smells lingering in the air, the beauty of uniqueness. How about water? Running water, cold water, hot water, any water. It's all miraculous! If we can stop seeing things as mundane, normal, and routine, the natural world becomes the supernatural, and it will absolutely change our lives. This will uncap the lid of expectancy in our lives.

> LIVING OUT GOD'S GREATNESS IS A WHOLE LOT EASIER WHEN WE SEE IT ALL AROUND US, WHEN WE REALIZE THAT HIS GREATNESS IS EVERYWHERE IN EVERYTHING.

It will take us to a new level of living. Living out God's greatness is a whole lot easier when we see it all around us, when we realize that His greatness is everywhere in everything. It's like peeling back an orange. When you get the bitter covering peeled back, you can experience the sweetness of the fruit. Even better, once you eat the fruit and get to the center of it, you're left with a seed, something to plant, something to tend, creating more fruit when planted, producing more seed, generating more of a harvest.

Let's peel back our bitterness, our toughness (those invisible walls that we've erected in response to the hard things in life we've experienced), and instead, enjoy everything God has placed around us. Let's live in such a way that our lives begin to produce more fruit, adding to the harvest of Heaven.

I'm just one example of how God can help us peel back our layers and begin to see Him in new, fresh ways. I regularly feel outrageously blessed by his greatness in something seemingly ordinary, like one of my kids' smiles from across a room, the sun rising, or the leaves of a tree rustling in the wind outside my kitchen window.

I notice it in the echoing laughs of one too many kids packed in our pool or a simple hot cup of coffee in my hand.

It may be in a simple yet meaningful gesture, a random act of kindness, or watching an old couple walking hand in hand. It can be found in the crashing waves of the ocean or in the tiniest grains of sand. It's barefoot summers and fishing at the creek with my kids. It's ice cream stops and bike rides on the tandem. It's memories and dreams and the picture of my grandpa and grandma. It's Sunday lunches at my mom's and dad's after church; it's catching a glimpse of my hubby doing what he loves to do. It's laughing with our kids and eating dinner together, whether at the table or in the car. It's the summer garden and the winter snow (Okay, the snow is beautiful, but I hate the cold. I have no idea why we live here!).

MY HEART LONGS FOR YOU TO EXPERIENCE THIS ADVENTURE, A LIFE LIVING OUT THE GREATNESS OF YOUR CREATOR. THERE IS NOTHING LIKE IT IN THE WHOLE WORLD.

All these moments fill my heart and soul. They do something inside me that I can hardly put into words. What I've come to realize is that each one of these are daily reminders, a glimpse of God's greatness at work.

These things bring me joy. I may not be able to explain it eloquently, but my heart longs for you to experience this adventure, a life living out the greatness of your Creator. There is nothing like it in the whole world.

It's time we begin to experience the little things as well as the big things that God has for us, the little moments of joy, the things that pull on your heartstrings, moments that inspire, motivate, and challenge you, experiences and opportunities that will flip your world inside out.

Things that dare your soul to dream bigger and do more.

Seasons that put into perspective what truly matters in this crazy thing we call life. God's greatness is wrapped up in a million different ways. Some gifts are huge, and some are small. Some last forever and some are seasonal. Some gifts are people, and some are things. Some are mere moments, and others are lifelong companions following us forever into eternity. Some are packed with awesome stuff, literally physical, tangible items. Yet others, when unwrapped, make the stuff seem so small in comparison. In my opinion, those gifts are the best. Some gifts are meant just for you, and others are to be shared. Some you experience immediately, and others are wrapped in 47 boxes. You open one only to find another layer, another box, but it's often in the smallest, most tedious gifts unwrapped that you'll find the greatest treasures.

THE MOST ANNOYING SOUND EVER

Recently, I was in the car with my hubby and kiddos, reading a book as we were driving down this long, monotonous stretch of road that we must drive in order to get anywhere from our little village. It was quite blissful. I disappeared into a place I'll refer to as "me" mode. It was my own world with just me, my book, and the sun's rays pressing through the window warming my face. It was glorious. Then, out of nowhere, I heard an ear-piercing sound. It was absolutely horrific to experience. It made me cringe, and it immediately caused me to begin desperately begging the little human (who I quickly discovered was the source of the outrageous noise) in the back seat to stop. Once the atrocious scream came to a halt, the whole car busted out laughing. Everyone except me, that is. Who would laugh at that? It was debilitating and detesting to the ears.

Little did I know, in my moments of "me" mode, the rest of the family decided to have a "who can make the most annoying sound ever" contest, and so the annoying sounds continued for the next half hour.

I fought the idea hard for the first few minutes until I found myself sucked into their laughter, making annoying sounds of my own.

I share this to say don't miss the miraculous.

Don't miss those moments, my friends. Stop and soak them in. Life is way too short to not stop, laugh, and make the most annoying sound ever. At first glance, who would think that an annoying sound was a blessing? But, after I took a second look and saw the laughter those crazy noises were inducing, I found joy. And, I had a choice to make, be annoyed because my "me" time was interrupted and perhaps ruin their fun or enjoy this silly moment with my family and laugh my butt off. All, I needed to do was shift my perspective to see things differently—uncover a blessing in disguise.

We must fix our eyes on the good, the beautiful, and the lovely, even in the seasons when we may have to search for them. If we choose to see the good, we'll begin to find it everywhere.

Maybe it's in your conversations with Jesus, your family, or your friends. Possibly tucked inside your memories and dreams, your purpose and your passions. It's learning through moments of pure pain and heartache that even if we can't understand it all, we know without a doubt that God is good.

He has spoken to me, comforted me, encouraged my heart, and lifted my head more than any earthly vessel could.

> IF WE CHOOSE TO SEE THE GOOD, WE'LL BEGIN TO FIND IT EVERYWHERE.

He knows me better than I know myself and believes in me more than I could ever hope another could. He talks to me, opens doors for me, and thank goodness, He closes some.

Bottom line: Keep your eyes fixed on Jesus. Expect the greatness of God to consume you, even when you don't feel like it. Do it. What you're going through may not make sense but be confident He will see you through.

Do you remember how I asked God in the beginning of this journey how on earth I was supposed to help people to expect His greatness? I mean, I had no idea where to start except for doing it myself.

I recently heard a phrase, and it hasn't released its grip on my head and heart. From the time I heard it, I knew it was the Holy Spirit saying, "This is how you can teach people to expect my greatness."

The phrase was one I mentioned earlier.

Live it so loud that they crave it.

Live Jesus so loud that people crave Him. Live expecting God's greatness in such a way that people desire it for themselves. There is a story in the book of Joel that screams truth into this phrase.

It is an interesting book. It's about Joel, who was an Old Testament prophet in his day. His prophecy carries some heavy words and difficult truths, but there is a line in this book that has pressed its fingerprint into my soul.

Joel 2:17b (ESV) says,

"Why should they say among the peoples, 'Where is their God?'"

> LIVE JESUS SO LOUD THAT PEOPLE CRAVE HIM. LIVE EXPECTING GOD'S GREATNESS IN SUCH A WAY THAT PEOPLE DESIRE IT FOR THEMSELVES.

Here's what was going on: Joel was warning the people about what was currently taking place in their land. He also was notifying them about what was to come. He was telling them about the things they've experienced and that soon, everything was going to be gone. The grain was going to become withered, animals would cry out with groans, flames would devour the orchards, and the river would even begin to dry up and shrivel. The storehouses would be in ruin, and the food supplies would be cut off.

So, Joel gathers His people. He brings them together and issues a call of repentance. He says, "Come on, bring an offering with you into the house of the Lord. Cry out to God Almighty. Fast, pray, repent." (Joel 1:13-14 NIV)

He goes on to tell of all the things that will come, and it gets heavy, but then he says it. He says, "Why should they say among the peoples, 'Where is their God?'"

Ultimately, he was saying, "We are the children of God. Are we really going to sit here and let people question the ability, the love, and the favor of our God? Why are we content serving the God of the impossible yet expecting less than His best? Nothing is impossible with God."

> WHY ARE WE CONTENT SERVING THE GOD OF THE IMPOSSIBLE YET EXPECTING LESS THAN HIS BEST? NOTHING IS IMPOSSIBLE WITH GOD.

Let me ask you this: Would people in your life right now say, "Where is your God?" Can they say that about you? If so, enough! That's exactly what the Enemy wants. Enough! Let them see that your God is active, alive, and present in your life. Let them see He is there amid your situation, equipping, guiding, taking the impossible and making it possible. Expect His greatness.

What if we lived our lives in such a way that people looking from the outside in would say not "Where is her God?" but rather, "Who is her God? Who is his God? How can I get what they have? How can I get my hands on that peace, that joy, that purpose? Who is it that they serve? Who is that God of miracles, protection, and favor? I want that; I want their God. How do they do what they do and have what they have? Why is their family different, their kids, their marriage, their work? Who is their God?"

Can you imagine? Is your heart beating a little faster? Are your palms beginning to sweat? Are you getting excited at the thought, the possibility of what living a life expecting and experiencing God's greatness can do?

Now, maybe you're already experiencing a life like that. If so, then I'm sure you would agree with the statement below.

A life like this doesn't simply happen. It takes intention; it takes discipline.

I am probably one of the most laid-back people on the planet. I've always been comfortable with taking the back seat. It's natural for me to sit back and stay quiet. I like to watch and observe. It's how I'm wired. Naturally, I wasn't equipped with a take-charge, expectant personality. It took discipline and spiritual equipping. I had to learn to make new pathways in my mind, and it took intention. It was not easy for me; I had to work at it and still do.

Let me explain. Through one of the darkest, most trying seasons of my life, I experienced first-hand moments where the people who I thought would have and should have exemplified Jesus to me seemed to possess the opposite of His characteristics. It frustrated me and confused me. It made me question the things God had planted deep in my Spirit. It made me rethink all He was speaking over me.

I was hurt; I felt abandoned. But again, God spoke into that pain. He helped me understand I was taking the back seat and that was not what He had been equipping me to do. He spoke and said, "Show them My greatness. Show them my love; show them my mercy and my grace. Show them my favor and my heart. Lift their heads and encourage them. Lead them, serve them, guide them. Be real with them. Let them in. Let them see that life may not be perfect, but my love is. It can be trusted. Fulfill the call, Dianne; be bold, confident, and courageous."

Here's what I learned: Living God's greatness may not always seem like a big deal. You will more than likely question its capabilities. You will wonder why living Him so loud is so hard; you'll wonder if it's making an impact at all and if anyone anywhere even notices. LISTEN TO ME. Being all God created you to be will not only change your life, but it will impact others for all of eternity. I promise you, His call, His purpose, His greatness will not fail you. People *will* say, "Who is their God?"

BEING ALL GOD CREATED YOU TO BE WILL NOT ONLY CHANGE YOUR LIFE, BUT IT WILL IMPACT OTHERS FOR ALL OF ETERNITY.

I literally cried typing this (man, I cry a lot!) because I was the least of these to live in this way. I am the person who never let anyone in. I'm the one who longed for peace and resolve at the cost of my battered heart.

I would fake a smile at all costs just to make people think everything was perfect. Because I had to hold it together. At least that's what I thought.

Friends, God doesn't expect perfection from us. This life is not perfect, and He doesn't expect us to walk around pretending it is. People can't relate to that type of religion. It's just not real or attainable.

THIS LIFE IS NOT PERFECT, AND HE DOESN'T EXPECT US TO WALK AROUND PRETENDING IT IS. PEOPLE CAN'T RELATE TO THAT TYPE OF RELIGION. IT'S JUST NOT REAL OR ATTAINABLE.

I could write a whole other book on my mistakes and bad choices, and to air it would do the majority no good at all. But if one, just one of those situations, stories, or bad choices could make an eternal impact, if it could encourage a struggling heart or bring triumph over the gnawing condemnation of the

Enemy, then game on. Pull the rug back and take your fill.

You see, so often we want to hide our past hurts, and we want to keep the living room of our lives so tidy that we brush all we are embarrassed or ashamed of under the rug so everything looks perfect. But last I checked, perfection never helped anyone. It actually eats us alive, filling our hearts with discontentment and comparison.

What the hearts of our brothers and sisters long for is authenticity. It's a relief to the human heart to know that others may have been or are currently as messed up as us and are still making it.

WHAT THE HEARTS OF OUR BROTHERS AND SISTERS LONG FOR IS AUTHENTICITY. IT'S A RELIEF TO THE HUMAN HEART TO KNOW THAT OTHERS MAY HAVE BEEN OR ARE CURRENTLY AS MESSED UP AS US AND ARE STILL MAKING IT.

I had to learn over the years to pull back the rug and confidently be authentically me, even if others don't love me for it or encourage me along the way. When I did that, I found freedom, not only for myself but for others as well. It was part of the equipping process.

REAL OR RAW

Don't you think the human soul craves authenticity? I believe it does, especially in a world of microwave foods and GMOs.

I mean, how many of us get excited at the thought of a home-cooked meal enjoyed around the table with the ones we love most?

Imperfections and all!

I was at a dinner party the other night; the hostess burned the main dish, and I was like, "Thank you, thank you for burning that. Because now I don't feel so bad for my epic dinner party fails."

Seriously, I've had some dupes. But, understanding that no one really has it "all" together, relaxes us and it puts things into perspective. No one is perfect, and if they seem to be, you just don't know them all that well.

So, friends, take the pressure off.

I'm sure I'm not the only one who shoves nine loads of dirty laundry into my closet before company comes over. I've even hidden dirty clothes in the dryer before. Later, when it came time to fold, hopefully, I remembered they were dirty.

I've packed the dishwasher double full just to clean out the sink, and I've even resorted to putting things in the back of my car with a whim's notice of someone stopping by.

Why? Because there is this crazy drive in us to always look perfect and put together. We always want to leave people thinking, *wow, how do they keep everything so clean and tidy? How do they always look put together? How are their kids so well behaved?*

Well, here's a truth bomb: my house isn't always clean. Actually, it's hardly ever super clean, except for when I am planning on people coming over, but even then, within a few hours, it looks just like it did before people arrived. I'm really not all that put together. I have to wear hats much more than I prefer because I rarely remember to make a hair appointment, and after 40, let's just say hair appointments are needed.

The truth is we are all so much alike. How many of you, like me, wear your pajamas or yoga pants far too long into the day and dry shampoo has become just as important to you as your morning cup of joe? I mean, at this exact moment, its two o'clock in the afternoon. I'm sitting at my desk in my basement, my unwashed hair is in a bun. I haven't showered, hence the unwashed hair. I have on a pair of yoga pants that are at least 8 years old; I'm wearing my husband's high school football sweatshirt (Um, he's 42 if that gives you a clue to how old this shirt is). I'm currently wiping snot on the sleeves of this sweatshirt because while writing, I began to reminisce about my sweet daddy who we just lost 3 weeks ago. Life is messy, and right now, I'm messy. So there, for those of you who assumed that when one writes a book, they are dressed and ready, beautiful and confident, and have everything figured out, um… wrong. This is the reality—true confessions of a writer.

Here's the deal, stop putting the pressure on yourself to be perfect and focus on being relational. Authentically be the best version of you, and just go do what you are called to do, even if you do it while wiping snot into your sleeves. It's okay!

People need you. They need your voice, your confidence, and your courage. They need your example. They need Jesus doing what He does best in and through you! God wants you to be authentic, He is giving you permission to be yourself, and this is just another one of His precious gifts to unwrap. To find yourself in the presence of the One who wants you to be who you really are. The One who loves you just as you are. The One who designed you, your face, body shape,

AUTHENTICALLY BE THE BEST VERSION OF YOU, AND JUST GO DO WHAT YOU ARE CALLED TO DO, EVEN IF YOU DO IT WHILE WIPING SNOT INTO YOUR SLEEVES. IT'S OKAY!

personality, and gave you your strengths. To be not only allowed but encouraged to be fully you is a gift. And again, as you open this gift of authenticity, you inspire others to be authentic. Open this gift and pass it out to everyone you meet.

In this Pinterest-perfect age we live in, the world needs authentic people. Yes, show your strengths and the beauty you can create, but also, don't be afraid to showcase when you don't have it all together! Will the Pinterest-fail people please stand up?!

PEOPLE NEED YOU. THEY NEED YOUR VOICE, YOUR CONFIDENCE, AND YOUR COURAGE. THEY NEED YOUR EXAMPLE. THEY NEED JESUS DOING WHAT HE DOES BEST IN AND THROUGH YOU!

Authenticity speaks volumes in our everyday lives. It's yet another way we can begin to teach people that it's okay to expect God's greatness. He longs for us to be authentically us because it's what allows us to live Him so loud that others crave the One we have.

8

Getting Hung Up

AND I'M NOT TALKING ABOUT LAUNDRY

What's the worst first impression you have ever experienced of another person? Or, worse yet, what's the worst first impression you've ever given of yourself?

It was literally just a few weeks ago, just three days after losing my dad that I'm convinced I must have left one of the most memorable first impressions ever. It was a Sunday morning, and we had a million things to do in preparation for the week to come. I was a mess, a rollercoaster of emotions, but I had to get some things checked off my to-do list. In the meantime, my hubby decided it would be the perfect Sunday to check out this church that some friends of ours told us about since we would be out that way. I'm not going to lie, I was mad. The last thing I wanted to do was go to a new church, meet new people, smile, and be friendly. I was sad, and I missed my dad.

But I went with the agreement that we would sit near the back. Oh my goodness, it was horrible. The church was great, but every single song talked about death and the tomb, and the message was titled, "Finding Joy in the Pain." What?!?!?! I understand there is joy to be found, later. I was not ready for it being only three days into the very depth of that pain. I just wasn't ready. But, I did it; I held back my sobbing for the whole service until they started singing the closing worship song. It was beautiful, it was like Jesus was coming down and wrapping his arms around me, and I was breaking, in a good way, but the floodgates were about to open. So, I desperately said to my husband, "Give me the keys!" Of course, he didn't hear me above the music, so I yelled, "Give me the keys!"

He responded, "Do you want me to come with you?" I could not speak in this moment. Remember, I'm about to burst into an uncontrollable meltdown; like a real hardcore grieving cry.

So, I yell (literally, I'm being very loud, I just couldn't help it), "No, just give me your keys!"

Now, if that didn't make an impression on those around me, then I don't know what would have, but wait, it gets better! Remember, I've never been to this place before, so I walk out of the sanctuary and go to exit through the two big glass doors standing before me only to find a sign hanging that said, "Emergency Exit Only." AHHH!!!!! I did not have time for this. So, with tears flowing down my cheeks, keys in hand, and frantically searching through my purse for my sunglasses to cover my black mascara covered face, I look to the nearest greeter who was obviously frazzled by my looks, and I say, "How do I get out of this place?" Oh, that poor guy.

He was so taken aback. He said, "Umm, I'm so sorry, what?"

I replied, "I can't get out those doors. I need to get out of here; how do I get out of this place?"

You guys, seriously, it was as dramatic as it sounds. Probably even more so. That poor man, frazzled and all, showed me to the real exit doors, and I bolted, tears flowing. I mean, can you imagine that first impression? I'm sure I left a mark on that man's mind. Poor guy!

The reality is you never get a second chance to make a first impression.

To add to that pressure, seven seconds is all you have.

Just google it. It only takes seven seconds for you to make a first impression on another human being. That's it. Seven measly seconds.

There are enough stats and percentages in that topic to keep you busy for months, but what jumped out at me immediately is that we get so hung up on what we feel or notice in the first few seconds that often, we never really get to know the depths of many people, situations, or opportunities. Why? Because we've simply made our mind up in a whole seven seconds.

A question started to linger in my thoughts after reading on this topic. I couldn't help but wonder, what we are missing out on? Imagine how much more there is to that person we've written off or that business opportunity that we quit listening to after the first two words because it sounds like a pyramid, or the possible friendships we've dismissed because the person looked or sounded differently. What are we missing out on? What situations could have blessed us? What opportunities could have grown us? What relationships could have led us, challenged us, or loved us through life if we hadn't turned away after only seven seconds of their time?

The reality is we often dismiss what we don't understand or relate with. If something seems too good to be true or too unusual, then we tend to put it in the "do not explore any further" category. We get hung up on normal and comfortable.

This whole first impression thing makes me think of that beautiful banquet room again. Not because of the missed relationships or the opportunity necessarily, but because the Devil longs to get us caught up in logic and wrapped up in comfort and worldly reality. He does this so that the first impression of the banquet room and the ridiculously grand table of gifts, in our minds, get the boot to the category of "do not explore any further."

He will whisper lies like:

"You don't deserve it."

"These gifts are a façade, too good to be true."

"If you go for them, you're just going to get hurt again."

"If God has such greatness for you, then why have you had such a hard time?"

Friends, this is tough ground to cover, but listen to me; these are all heart wrenching, dark, heavy, deceitful lies of the Enemy.

If you have a wall, the Devil will deceive you into thinking that you can't get the wall down.

If you don't have a wall but haven't approached your table yet, the devil still has you where he wants you, wallowing around in the "I don't deserve all of this" stage.

Don't let the curse of envy, abuse, neglect, brokenness, depression, anxiety, divorce, sickness, addiction, poverty mentality, or anything else keep you from your table. There is freedom sitting there waiting to break those chains of bondage. Speak God's truth over your situation. Break the curses and strongholds, those generational issues in the name of Jesus.

Freedom is yours for the taking. Don't just pretend the problems and the pain didn't happen or don't exist. Speak life into them.

FREEDOM IS YOURS FOR THE TAKING. DON'T JUST PRETEND THE PROBLEMS AND THE PAIN DIDN'T HAPPEN OR DON'T EXIST. SPEAK LIFE INTO THEM.

Oh Lord, how my heart longs so desperately for the truth to be revealed right now in this moment. Let your truth ring loud and clear in the heart and mind of every reader that needs this. Lord, shatter walls with your truth, right now in this very moment. Let them fall to the ground, destroyed in such a way that they may never be put back together again. Shatter walls, Lord; strike them with Your truth.

KEEP THAT UGLY DOWN

Two things affect so much of what we do, possibly every action or reaction we make: discipline and self-control.

Think about it. Every choice to speak, not to speak, respond, not respond, they take self-control and discipline. Every decision, every bite we take, goal we set, every dream we dream, and wish we wish are 100% determined by our self-discipline and our self-control.

ARE WE WILLING TO BE DISCIPLINED TO GET WHAT WE WANT? ARE WE WILLING TO SACRIFICE WHAT WE WANT NOW TO PURSUE BECOMING ALL WE WERE CREATED TO BE? ARE WE WILLING TO GO AGAINST THE WORLD AND TRUST OUR CREATOR FOR ALL HE SAYS HE IS?

Are we willing to be disciplined to get what we want? Are we willing to sacrifice what we want now to pursue becoming all we were created to be? Are we willing to go against the world and trust our Creator for all He says He is?

Are you?

I believe God wants the best for each and every one of us. This may seem a little out in left field, but that's okay. I like left field. It often holds the unexpected.

Remember how I had to learn some things and unlearn other things? Here's one verse that I had to unlearn from a wrong perspective and relearn to believe it to be true for me.

It's found in John 14:12-14 (ESV).

"Truly, truly, I say to you, whoever believes in me will also do the works that I do; and greater works than these will he do, because I am going to the Father. Whatever you ask in my name, this I will do, that the Father may be glorified in the Son. If you ask me anything in my name, I will do it."

This is almost too much for our beautiful minds to comprehend. Seriously, "...whoever believes in me will also do the works that I do..." But, that's not it. It gets even better. Now, remember, these are the words of Jesus, the King of Kings and the Lord of Lords. You see, there is a major reason why He's making this statement, this commitment, this promise.

He says, "... this I will do, THAT the Father (God Himself) may be glorified in the Son" (emphasis added).

So, get this, friend. So often, we breeze by or skip over these thought-proving, faith-building, too-good-to-be-true scriptures because of two major issues that tend to keep us from experiencing Jesus's promise for us.

1. We simply don't believe it.

Our human tendency longs for everything to make sense and for the ability to comprehend all the scriptures say. God simply isn't something we can comprehend. How dare we not believe things based on man's logical explanation, with the reasoning that if it's too good to be true, then it probably is. Jesus and what He did for us does sound too good to be true, but HE IS TRUE and what HE DID FOR US IS TRUE! We can't earn His sacrifice; we don't deserve His sacrifice. But, He gave himself away freely to set us free. He was loyal, even though He knew we wouldn't always be. None of it makes any logical sense.

> OUR UNBELIEF IN WHAT GOD CAN DO IN AND THROUGH US IS THE ONLY THING THAT LIMITS US.

But to be honest neither does most of the world we live in. I mean, just look at the moon. It's crazy awesome, and it's only by the power of God himself that it's there hanging in the darkened sky every, single, night. God is too great to comprehend, but that doesn't change that His Word is true, even if it seems too good. Now, take all of the too-good-to-be-true promises in the Bible and simply believe them. Believe them to be true for you. Our unbelief in what God can do in and through us is the only thing that limits us.

Let's look at 2 Kings 4:1-6 (NIV):

The wife of a man from the company of the prophets cried out to Elisha, "Your servant my husband is dead, and you know that he revered the Lord. But now his creditor is coming to take my two boys as his slaves."

Elisha replied to her, "How can I help you? Tell me, what do you have in your house?"

"Your servant has nothing there at all," she said, "except a small jar of olive oil." Elisha said, "Go around and ask all your neighbors for empty jars. Don't ask for just a few. Then go inside and shut the door behind you and your sons. Pour oil into all the jars, and as each is filled, put it to one side."

She left him and shut the door behind her and her sons. They brought the jars to her and she kept pouring. When all the jars were full, she said to her son, "Bring me another one."

But he replied, "There is not a jar left." Then the oil stopped flowing.

This woman was going to lose her sons. She was stuck and felt there was no way out. The situation seemed hopeless. That is until Elisha (a prophet of God) told her what to do. He told her to go borrow as many jars as she could. He specifically said, "[Let] it not be few," meaning, this is going to be good. Be prepared. Be ready; get what you need lined up to receive all that God has for you. Believe that God's greatness will fall on you and fill whatever you have.

This woman had to believe and do what Elisha told her to do. She couldn't risk using her human logic here and neither can we. When our human logic tries to go head-to-head with our Creator's infinite greatness whose thoughts, plans, and ways cannot be comprehended by our little finite mindsets, we end up capping our blessing. Why? Because the created being can't possibly outthink, explain, or comprehend the mindset of the Creator?

Just like this woman had to believe and trust in Elisha's instructions, we too have put our trust and hope in God and believe His Word to be true for us. If this lady, this widow would have brought one jar, the greatness of God would have filled it. If she had five jars, He would have filled it. But if she had the faith to bring fifty jars or five hundred jars, guess what? The greatness of God would have not been capped, and He would have filled each and every jar she laid before Him.

So, ask yourself, what are you "capping"? What possible blessing, miracle, or dream are you putting the cap or lid on due to your use of human logic? Are you taking the greatness of God and all He has for you and twisting it tightly closed and setting it on the shelf because it may not be logical in your mind? Or are you approaching the King of Kings with an expectant heart, standing before Him ready to unleash your faith and dive into every single gift, blessing, and miracle He has for you? Are you believing His greatness to be true for you? Are you believing your marriage to be restored, your business to surpass anything you ever dreamed or imagined? Are you expecting His healing power or His financial provision? If you do, He flips your world upside down and inside out, just like He did for this widow and her sons. I dare you to simply try it.

Check out 2 Kings 4:7 (NIV):

"She went and told the man of God, and he said, 'Go, sell the oil and pay your debts. You and your sons can live on what is left.'"

TWO GENERATIONS OF BLESSINGS IN ONE ACT OF FAITHFUL OBEDIENCE. WHAT IS GOD ASKING YOU TO DO?

Here are a family and a mom who went from having nothing but a little jar of oil to never having to work another day in their lives. And not just her, but her sons as well. She broke her wall of impossibility and trusted God's direction. Two generations of blessings in one act of faithful obedience. What is God asking you to do?

2. We let fear rule us.

Another sneaky seed of the Enemy is fear. Fear keeps so many of God's children rocking back and forth in the fetal position of defeat, feeling trapped with no way out. Fear is just another lie of the Enemy plastered across the walls of so many keeping them from all God has for them. Jesus' glorious work on the cross defeated the Enemy. He has no authority over you except what you give him. Jesus took back the keys so you could be free. He suffered an unthinkable, incomprehensible death so you and I could have victory.

I'm passionate about this because it is something the Enemy lied to me about for way too long. I'm sick and tired of him keeping you and others from their God-given authority. He lies and deceives because that's all he has; He only has lies. He has NO authority any longer over the Christ-follower. So, for the love of all that is holy, STOP GIVING HIM BACK THE KEYS!!!! Stop making agreements with him in the area of fear.

You are not called to live afraid.

The Word of God says DO NOT FEAR. It's a message woven through the entire Bible, a mandate reiterated time and time again. Do you think maybe God knew His children would have a bit of a struggle in this area? I know I did for a long time, but I rebuke fear daily. I refuse to give fear an ounce of space in my brain. We have kingdom things to think on; Fear holds us back from furthering the purposes of God. We must stop agreeing in fear with the Enemy. I believe with all my heart that there are a slew of Christ-following, Jesus-loving, kingdom-building rockstars out there who believe wholeheartedly the scripture we talked about in John 14:12, but I think many of them are scared to death that it could be true for them.

Let me explain.

It can be a bit overwhelming to think that God is willing to use us to do the same things that His perfect son Jesus did (John 14:12-14). The Devil wants you to feel ashamed you would even consider the thought of doing something as amazing as what Jesus did when He walked the earth. He whispers things like, "Who are you to believe God could use you? You're so far from perfect. You're not good enough, or you're reading into this wrong. Like God would allow you to do things that Jesus did." I used to assure myself that there had to be a deeper meaning to this John 14 verse, a hidden secret I wasn't getting. Thinking, *surely, He's not going to use me to perform miracles.* But I had to retrain my thoughts to take God at His Word and know that it applied to me, and He meant what He said!

If we don't instantly take these negative, reluctant thoughts captive and kick them out of our head, we will have yet again made agreements with the Enemy in the area of fear. Agreements like:

Fear of failure

Fear of worth

Fear of attack (so many of us are afraid that if we move forward with God's call, the Enemy is going to attack us even more so. The enemy only has this authority if we give it to him.)

Fear of success (yes, success)

Fear of the unknown

Fear of other people's thoughts and opinions

I had to retype some of this because as I was writing, I was gripped with the fear (momentarily, until I served that thought an eviction notice) of what some people might say about this chapter of my book. I had to dig down deep and be re-

I HAD TO DIG DOWN DEEP AND BE REMINDED THAT I'VE BEEN SET FREE FROM THE "RELIGION" OF JESUS, AND I'VE MADE MY HOME IN A TRUE "RELATIONSHIP" WITH JESUS THIS SHIFT HAS GIVEN ME A FREEDOM AND CONFIDENCE I NEVER KNEW EXISTED.

minded that I've been set free from the "religion" of Jesus, and I've made my home in a true "relationship" with Jesus—this shift has given me a freedom and confidence I never knew existed. I mean, part of me feels like I'm going to need to apologize for saying this, but I'm not going to. If living for Jesus must be "culturally" acceptable, then I don't want it. I don't want cultural Christianity. I want God, Jesus, and the Holy Spirit. That's it, that's all. Cultural Christianity is capped by comfort, fear, unbelief, and opinions of others. Basically, it's a religion that is comfortable and selfish.

I'm sick of being comfortable.

What great things come from comfort? Can you think of one? If comfort or the fear of moving and doing is a cap on God's greatness, His provision, His call, His blessing, His favor, His plan of redemption and love for the lost, then I don't want comfort. Am I tempted by it? You bet I am, but my soul longs too much for Him and His ways. Let's refuse to let fear of God's greatness keep us from receiving it. Together, let's kick the Devil in the face with our expectant hearts and take authority, receiving all God has for us.

CULTURAL CHRISTIANITY IS CAPPED BY COMFORT, FEAR, UNBELIEF, AND OPINIONS OF OTHERS. BASICALLY, IT'S A RELIGION THAT IS COMFORTABLE AND SELFISH.

FIGHTING FEAR

I'm over the Enemy pushing people around with fear. Turn on the TV and some newscaster somewhere is getting paid to pump you full of worry. Read the paper, watch a movie, talk to another human, the devil's deceit is everywhere, and it's masked as fear. Rip it off, my friends. Rip. It. Off.

But, how?

I don't have all the answers, but I do have a testimony. I can tell how I've learned to overcome various fears in my life and shatter the barrier that kept me from experiencing God's best. First, I learned to wield weapons that would combat it.

EVERY SPIRIT-BREATHED, INSPIRED WORD IS A TOOL GOD HAS GIVEN US TO TEAR DOWN STRONGHOLDS AND LIES.

If we are not armed and equipped with this weapon, the sword of the Spirit, God's Word, then we're in trouble. Understanding the power of God's word is another one of God's gifts to us. It is a gift of highest value and it sits, waiting, prepared on His banquet table. Once we choose to unwrap this gift and realize how absolutely essential it is to live a victorious and free life, we'll never, ever look at the Bible the same. Every Spirit-breathed, inspired word is a tool God has given us to tear down strongholds and lies. Using the Word of God and applying the abundant truths and promises to break down piece after piece of that glass wall and open us up to powerful living. We must know our enemy and know how to hit him hard. Otherwise, he slithers in, and suddenly, we find ourselves intimidated by the great things God has for us, our gifts. I know people who are scared to death of being wealthy. Now, I understand that some people maybe couldn't handle financial provision, but a God-fearing, Jesus-loving, kingdom-building soul should not be scared of financial blessings. God can use wealth in a mighty way. Fear like this is a blow from the Enemy. Too many whispers from him make people question the blessing of God's favor. Here are some scriptures that I've armed myself with to help me overcome these whispers:

2 Corinthians 10:3-5 (ESV)
"For though we walk in the flesh, we are not waging war according to the flesh. For the weapons of our warfare are not of the flesh but have divine power to destroy strongholds. We destroy arguments and every lofty opinion raised against the knowledge of God and take every thought captive to obey Christ."

Paul is saying that this is not a flesh battle; it's a spiritual one. The weapons of this warfare are not physical but spiritual. We must fight with prayer, the Word of God, praise, faith, and the power of the Holy Spirit. We must do our part. We must use our armor and our weapons.

We must destroy the arguments that go against the Word of God. We must take every thought captive and, if it fails to align with God's Word, we have to throw it out. We can not afford to have thoughts of the evil one linger in our heads, because if we do, they make their way to our hearts.

God is so good; He makes things so clear. Check out Philippians 4:8 (NIV) where He tells us what to think on through the words of Paul:

"Finally, brothers and sisters, whatever is true, whatever is noble, whatever is right, whatever is pure, whatever is lovely, whatever is admirable—if anything is excellent or praiseworthy —think about such things."

WE CAN NOT AFFORD TO HAVE THOUGHTS OF THE EVIL ONE LINGER IN OUR HEADS, BECAUSE IF WE DO, THEY MAKE THEIR WAY TO OUR HEARTS.

We have to take our thoughts captive, each one of them. Then, we must analyze them and hold them up to the truth in Philippians 4:8. If it does not align, throw that sucker out. Get rid of it. Refuse to ponder on it or give it another second of power. Kick it to the curb! Does that overwhelm you a bit? Take that up with Him, but if you need a confidence boost, guidance, or just a little help, simply ask the Holy Spirit to step in, lead you, and encourage you. He will!

Jesus himself says in John 10:27 (NIV), "My sheep listen to my voice; I know them and they follow me." His sheep know His voice. So, here's the gift of a lifetime: learning how to hear from God. It's one of the greatest gifts you'll ever unwrap. The Devil makes you want to question it. He wants you to think it was your thought and not God's. He tries to mess it all up.

LEARNING HOW TO HEAR FROM GOD. IT'S ONE OF THE GREATEST GIFTS YOU'LL EVER UNWRAP.

It's a process, part of the whole relationship thing, but through each and every conversation with God, prayer, and petition, His voice will become more and more clear. It's also important to know that God's voice manifests in different ways (Since not all are hearers.) It could be through His Word, it could be through a worship song, another person, you may be a "feeler", where God gives you a sense of what to do, or you might be a "see-er", and you hear from God visually or through a dream. Hearing from God is one of the most beautiful, breathtaking, exhilarating experiences one can ever have. I encourage you to spend time with the Lord, pour over the scriptures, and learn His word.

Here's my tactic. If I think God spoke something to me, I roll with it. I move, and if it wasn't Him, then I'm only one step closer to learning His voice even better. He won't be mad at you; He'll say, "Here's my voice again. Keep trying; you'll learn it." He wants you to learn His voice. For the love, could we all just stop thinking God is hovering over us with a beating stick waiting to crack us over the head every time we move forward and try? He's cheering you on. He's walking with you. He's got you; you're His baby girl or His precious son. He's so proud of you.

Why is it that so many fear God's greatness? Think about yourself and your situation. What scares you? If taking inventory of your situation shows an excess in the fear category, then you need to get some things straightened out. Number one: fear is not from God. He is not a God of fear and intimidation. Those characteristics don't belong to Him.

Let's analyze the fear of worrying about what others think. I waded my feet in the pool of other peoples' opinions for far too long. This took me a while to learn, but in my life, it was usually the most selfish things that I was afraid of, simply because my fear was often rooted in the thoughts of others. Someone once said to me, "Dianne, when you're constantly worried about pleasing everyone else, you're really just being selfish."

I was astounded. I thought my fear of being authentic was a way of me being kind to others. I didn't want to step on anyone's toes or ruffle anyone's feathers, so I would just do my best to keep everyone happy. Now, after being confronted with truth, I probably leave quite a few frolicking around trying to regroup and re-groom now that I've learned to embrace myself. The reality is when we mask our true selves in order to please those around us, what we are really saying is that we are fearful of what everyone else thinks. It's selfish in the sense that we worry more about how we are perceived than the actual feelings of others. It is selfishness masked as people-pleasing. We simply please people, so we look good. I know this is tough to hear but take it from a previous chronic people-pleaser, it's so not worth it.

You will never be all you were created to be; you'll never reach your destiny pleasing the world. You only have one person to please, and His name is Jesus. It takes so much pressure off. I promise, it's such a beautiful gift, learning to be authentically you, confidently and courageously. It's incredibly refreshing!

YOU WILL NEVER BE ALL YOU WERE CREATED TO BE; YOU'LL NEVER REACH YOUR DESTINY PLEASING THE WORLD.

Besides fear of what others would think of me, I was also afraid to lose my comfort. I touched on this earlier, but still, it's an extremely common fear. The enemy whispers, "You don't want that; you'll have to get up early, put even more hours in. You don't have time for that. You'll have to sacrifice your time, money and resources." He's sneaky with these lies. You have to learn to recognize your Father's voice and when thoughts are not from Him or fail to line up with His Word. Don't fall for these voices shouting at you. They are not truth.

Yes, you will have to sacrifice and give up comfort, but who cares when you are doing what you were created to do, living the life you were intended to live? All too often, I feel the current of comfort sucking me back into the sea of chaos that longs to swallow me whole. I want to write, but I have to get up earlier than I already do to fit it in my day. I have to carve out time here and there that would otherwise be filled with fun and family. It's way easier if I don't do it, don't let the call of comfort hook you. What motivates me is knowing that perhaps part of my story of breakthrough might lead others to find their own victory. I think, yes this may be hard, but boy, is it worth it. You're worth it.

> YOU WERE CREATED ON PURPOSE FOR A PURPOSE, BUT THAT DOESN'T MEAN YOU DON'T HAVE TO GET UNCOMFORTABLE AND WORK HARD TO MAKE THINGS HAPPEN.

I encourage you to expect God's greatness and get uncomfortable. It's good for you. You were created on purpose for a purpose, but that doesn't mean you don't have to get uncomfortable and work hard to make things happen. Live every minute of your life this way, and you will not regret a moment of it. It will be worth every sacrifice, eye roll, and doubt, every early morning and late night. Keep your eyes on the prize, your call, and your purpose, because He will do more than you could ever think, dream, or imagine. Trust me, I've seen the banquet table. It's amazing!

LET THAT UGLY WORK FOR YOU

Isaiah 61:3 (KJV) says, "To appoint unto them that mourn in Zion, to give unto them beauty for ashes, the oil of joy for the mourning, the garment of praise for the spirit of heaviness; that they might be called trees of righteousness, the planting of the Lord, that he might be glorified."

Isaiah is prophesying here. He's telling about what's to come. He's saying, listen, the Spirit of the Lord is upon me; He's appointed me to share some things, and I'm telling you, this is what the Lord's going to do. He's going to give you beauty for your ashes, joy for your mourning, and a garment, a covering of praise for your heaviness.

He's got you.

So, don't be ashamed of your ashes, your mourning, or your heaviness. All of that hurt will turn into beauty, joy, and praise. Tell others about your wall and how you broke it down with truth. There is power in your testimony. Show them that they, too, may experience beauty from their ashes.

> SO, DON'T BE ASHAMED OF YOUR ASHES, YOUR MOURNING, OR YOUR HEAVINESS. ALL OF THAT HURT WILL TURN INTO BEAUTY, JOY, AND PRAISE.

You've been through a lot, but God is about to take all that and give you beauty. Discern what is on your wall, break it down with God's truth, and take all the amazing gifts He has waiting.

9

Sailing the Sea

FOR THE LOVE, GET HIM IN YOUR BOAT!

It wasn't long ago, I was driving down the road I travel almost every day. I've driven this stretch of land more times than I can count over the last 20 years. As I was cruising along, this house that I had never seen before completely captured my attention. I was so confused because I could not remember a time when my eyes had fallen on that structure, yet it was anything but new. It was probably one of the oldest standing houses on the street. How could I have driven by this landscape for 20 years and never once noticed its existence? My first thought was how did that house get there? I would have undoubtedly noticed it if it had indeed always been here. But, sure enough, there it stood. It wasn't new, and no one randomly picked it up and placed it there.

It was just as it was, standing in that exact location since far before my birth.

I simply had never noticed it. Whether distracted by its lush landscape or having my attention pulled to the neighboring homes that tower on its left and right, I had failed to notice its existence.

Ironic maybe, but I prefer to give credit to my Creator. He literally gave me a physical real-life example to mirror the spiritual one that he allowed me to see in John 6:16-21 (ESV).

"When evening came, his disciples went down to the sea, got into a boat, and started across the sea to Capernaum. It was now dark, and Jesus had not yet come to them. The sea became rough because a strong wind was blowing. When they had rowed about three or four miles, they saw Jesus walking on the sea and coming near the boat, and they were frightened. But He said to them, 'It is I; do not be afraid.' Then they were glad to take him into the boat, and immediately the boat was at the land to which they were going."

Just like I had driven by that same house a million times, I have read this scripture more times than I can remember.

I've read and heard messages about Jesus walking on the water. I've read about Peter stepping out of the boat and walking toward Jesus on the waves, but in all my reading or instruction on this verse, I had never picked up on verse 21.

Oh my goodness, this is such a miraculous story. The miracle of Jesus walking on water is what most of us notice because it's indeed miraculous. Kind of like the houses that tower over the one I'd never noticed, the miracle of Jesus walking on water seems to tower over the miracle that's stood just as long as the one in verse 21.

Let me share it once again. John 6:21 says, "Then they were glad to take him into the boat, and immediately the boat was at the land to which they were going."

Did you pick up on it?

Let's back pedal just a few verses to set up the wonder in this miracle.

Here were Jesus' disciples. They've been walking with Jesus, talking with Jesus, and taking part in the miracles of Jesus. Here we find these men in a boat crossing the sea to Capernaum. Now, if we do a little research, we will find that the shortest distance in which they could have rowed across the sea would have been between 5-6 miles. Don't you find it interesting that the scripture clearly states that they had rowed about three or four miles out? Meaning they had at least one to two miles left to row.

Now, mind you, it's storming; the sea had become rough, and a strong wind was blowing.

How often do you feel like life is kicking your butt? You're a follower of Jesus; you walk with Him, talk with Him, and maybe you've even experienced a few miracles of His. Yet, you find yourself in a tough sea, being tossed around by the circumstances of life. You're okay, you're making it, but it's hard work. You're giving all you've got; you're rowing through the trudging waters as best you can. You may even have a few friends rowing with you, but you still have a ways to go. You still find yourself in the middle of the storm.

Throughout this book, I've challenged you to keep your eyes fixed on Jesus. Do that; it must stay a priority, but can I dare you to do something even more bold, more courageous?

In the midst of the storms, in the midst of the difficulties, the strong winds and the crashing waves, can I challenge you to do exactly what the disciples did in one of the most miraculous, yet overlooked, verses in the Bible?

In the middle of the storm, they not only fixed their eyes on Jesus, but they were glad to take Him in their boat and watch what happened. John 6:21(b), "...and immediately the boat was at the land to which they were going."

Remember, they still had up to two miles of rowing left when they saw Jesus.
When you invite Jesus into your boat, when you gladly bring Him on board, He can take you immediately to your destination. He can stop the storm, or he can immediately take you through it. Get Him in your boat. Bring Him in. Don't just fix your eyes on Him but invite Him gladly into your situation and surrender complete control.

As I sit here at my kitchen table, again, tears are falling to my keyboard because I hear God whisper, "If my kids will just bring me on board, if they will just trust me, if they will believe that I will do what I say I will do, if they fully surrender and believe my words to be true, Dianne, I can do the impossible. I can take my kids from raging seas instantaneously to peaceful shores."

I CAN TAKE MY KIDS FROM RAGING SEAS INSTANTANEOUSLY TO PEACEFUL SHORES.

Can you imagine what is possible if we take these words, focus on them, meditate on them, and then speak them into existence by faith, expecting God's Word to contain the same life-giving power He says it has? It's so simple. We overthink, over-articulate, confuse, and overwhelm people and ourselves with our own theology and our own thought processes about what really happens in life and how speaking God's Word can't possibly be enough.

I decided a long time ago to take God's Word just as it is written, to not over analyze what other people's thoughts and opinions were about it, but to just read it and allow the Holy Spirit to move, challenge, inspire, and encourage my faith. I wanted God Himself to speak to me through His Word. Now, do I listen to others? Yes, there are many wise minds in this world, some who lived long ago, some who we share life with, and others still yet to come. I absolutely allow myself to be taught, challenged, and encouraged by their teaching. The Holy Spirit works through people. I would just challenge you to keep personal time with your Creator, God almighty a priority. Don't just be filled by others. Make it a daily priority to get into the Word and grow your personal relationship with your Heavenly Father. Dive in, learn, and study God's Word. Take what others say and hold it up to what God's Word says.

At the end of this life, we stand before God, not our pastor, our friends, or even our families. Although, we may admire, respect, and highly esteem all of them, they cannot be our God. God is God.

Your table spread with limitless gifts is waiting. And, God wants you to experience every single one of them. You may have no idea what is in between His greatness for your life and you, but if you invite Him on your journey, if you ask Him to jump in your boat, He'll help make everything clear, in His timing. Trust Him with your journey, trust Him in the storms, trust that His Word is true, even if it doesn't match what you currently see. Having Jesus as our guide and helper is one of the best gifts we could ask for.

WHEN HE BRINGS YOU THROUGH THE STORM TO THE SHORE, YOU CAN CONFIDENTLY STAND YOUR GROUND!

Recently, I was talking to someone about what I feel God had been speaking to me, and to my dismay, this person was in complete disbelief.

This person said to me, "I want you to be very careful about what you tell me God said to you. I take that very seriously, and if God tells you something, you best not mess around. When God speaks, that's serious."

Now, I couldn't agree more, but that's not what saddened my heart. I shared with this person that God talks to me all the time. This person said, "Come on, God only talked to Abraham like six times. I'm pretty sure He's not talking to you that much." I was flabbergasted!

Here is my response, spoken in the most loving of ways:

"I am created in the image of God. His Word says so. I am the daughter of the King. God, the creator of the universe, is my Father. I am His daughter. That is my identity. I'm not a random human who has to tap into the supernatural power of God and hope that He'll converse with me. He's my Father. My loving, caring, gave-His-own-Son-up-for-me kind of Father. He loves me unconditionally, just as I am, but too much to leave me this way. He's my Daddy. And guess what? He talks to me."

I had such an array of emotions when this conversation started. It didn't take long for me to realize what was going on here. My eyes were opened even wider to the fact that there is a huge case of stolen identity in this world, and it's not just with the unbeliever. It's just as rampant in God's children, the ones who live their lives for Him. This identity thief isn't out to steal our bank accounts or our credit. This thief has come to steal the identity of God's children. He does all he can to make them think there is no real father-daughter or father-son relationship. He tries to blur the conversation, making us think that the communication lines only go one way, and every now and then, we may get a voicemail or a text from God with a next step or a "don't do that," but I refuse to believe that in the name of Jesus, and so should you. This is just another example of the dark lies that the enemy slathers our wall with. Making us think we have no real relationship with our Creator, that God doesn't speak to us, and if He does, we better watch out because it's void of grace. Oh how I pray that the words of truth shatter these lies in those who long to hear from their Daddy.

God is our father, and we have His Spirit living in us, not some random spirit that makes no difference in our world but the living Spirit of God. The Creator of the heavens and the earth, His Spirit lives in us.

THERE IS A HUGE CASE OF STOLEN IDENTITY IN THIS WORLD, AND IT'S NOT JUST WITH THE UNBELIEVER. IT'S JUST AS RAMPANT IN GOD'S CHILDREN, THE ONES WHO LIVE THEIR LIVES FOR HIM.

Jesus himself said that we were all going to be better off when He was gone because the Spirit would come. Might I add that Abraham didn't have what we have? Now, don't get me wrong, he walked and talked with God, but he was not a consistent dwelling place of the living Spirit of God. He didn't have access to what we have access to.

Friends, brothers, sisters, we are called to stop looking at the communication lines with our Father as one-way.

Stop thinking that He doesn't have things to share with you, hope to fill you with, dreams to move you, relationships to fill you and encourage you, gifts to bless others with, family and friends to support you, ministry to exude through you, healing to restore you.

He has so much for you. Communication is just one of the many gifts.

Start talking with Him. Remember that scripture I shared? He says that His sheep know His voice. Why would He say that if He was never going to talk to us?

God is urging us to build a relationship with Him, a one-on-one relationship. We need to grow and invest in it. We need to spend time with Him, learn His likes and dislikes, know when He speaks and how He speaks. We need to learn His communication styles and His love language. We spend all this time learning these things about people, but what have we learned about God?

Everything about God, Jesus, and the Holy Spirit is positive. By no means am I trying to say that theological training and education is a negative; it's 100% not bad in any way, shape, or form. It helps me tremendously, so thank you to all of those who have barreled through the endless hours of schooling and studying. I applaud you, as do many others. Thank you for your sacrifice and your lead.

What I'm trying to say is we can't fall back on other peoples' education and experience. We must have a personal, intimate relationship with our Creator.

What if I based my entire relationship with my husband completely on what other people told me they knew about him? That would be really crazy and rather weird. Why? Because no one knows my husband like I do, not his mother, his brother, or his best friend.

WE CAN'T FALL BACK ON OTHER PEOPLES' EDUCATION AND EXPERIENCE. WE MUST HAVE A PERSONAL, INTIMATE RELATIONSHIP WITH OUR CREATOR.

There is no other human being I have invested myself in more. There is no one that I've talked to more, no one that I'm more comfortable with or would rather be with. He knows more about me that any other human vessel on this planet, and he still loves me. We've worked through rough patches and enjoyed complete awesomeness together. We've worked hard and loved harder. I've invested in him, and he has invested in me. We are committed, no matter what.

It's no different with God our Father.

He does speak. I was so angry at the enemy for making one of God's kids think that He would have such little interest or desire to speak, communicate, and respond to them. I was mad that he had blurred their lines of communication.

I walked away from that conversation saying, "Lord, help me to help people understand Your heart. Help me to help them understand who You are as our Father." I can't imagine not hearing the voice of my heavenly Daddy. I can't imagine not knowing which way to go or turn, what steps to take or doors to walk through. A dad is supposed to cover and protect, lead and guide, challenge and inspire. They have to communicate with their child if they want to be effective. They have to stop and stoop down, look their daughter or their son in the eyes, and affirm their love and passion, their plan and their purpose.

Earthly fathers are going to fall short. They just will, and that's okay because our Heavenly Father never will. His voice may be louder or more constant in different seasons, but it's there. He's always there; His voice leads us and guides us. It's just the kind of Father that He is.

If you fail to hear the voice of God, get to know Him. He says you can learn His voice. The more time you spend with Him, the more you will begin to notice His gentle, soft whispers. His voice is never overbearing; you must pay attention and listen for it.

My challenge to you today is to learn to expect His voice; expect that your heavenly Father has something to say.

He is your Rock and your Fortress, your Healer and your Redeemer. He can be your Everything if you allow Him to use you, mold you, and guide you, if you allow Him to have His way in your life. He will use that to make an eternal impact, forging new lines in the future of your life. He will pour out His love and mercy, His grace and peace, in unimaginable ways. So, fix your eyes on Him; get Him in your boat. Approach your room with boldness and your table with tenacity. The Devil may try and stop you, lie about who you are, and who God is, but you are equipped with the sword of the Spirit. Simply slay him and his lies with the truth found in the Word of God.

As you journey towards experiencing all God has for you, value your time with Him. Seek deeper communication and expect to hear from your Creator. I can't even tell you how many times God has imparted wisdom and understanding, soft whispers and gentle nudges, downloaded new dreams and desires and challenged me to do different. The large majority of these moments happen when I'm in those quiet, secret places with Him, alone, reading, studying or just being still. So, do what you can to find those moments throughout your day. They are invaluable. Just start if you haven't already and continue to grow and invest in your relationship with your Heavenly Father. You won't regret a single second of it.

10

Get out of the Doorway

GO AHEAD, MOVE!

I am constantly asking God questions. I'm like a little kid asking a million and ten questions a day.

It wasn't too long ago that I was studying and praying about the kingdom of God. I find this topic fascinating and have so many things that I long to learn about it. One of the things that I was seeking wisdom on was about a line in the Lord's prayer. Mathew 6:10 (ESV) says: "Your kingdom come, your will be done on earth as it is in heaven."

So, I was like, Ok Lord, how is it that your kingdom come on earth like it is in Heaven? Help me to understand this. Your kingdom is perfection; it's where you are. It's where you reign and if your kingdom can be here, if I can dwell in that, then that's where I want to be. Immediately the banquet room popped into my mind, and it's like the Lord whispered, "You just have to step over the threshold. Everything I have is available to you. Everything I have is available to all of my kids."

You see, originally, I couldn't understand, after seeing the vision that I talked about in the beginning of this book and reading through scripture, why all of us don't just run up to our tables fearlessly. I didn't comprehend how some could miss the gifts altogether. But studying God's Word and the ways of His kingdom and praying through this vision and this whole book, I've learned that we need to be willing to step over the threshold of our reality into His realm. We must go beyond what we see and feel and be willing to train our brains, our words, and our beliefs. We must trust that which we cannot see and step into all He has for us.

WE NEED TO BE WILLING TO STEP OVER THE THRESHOLD OF OUR REALITY INTO HIS REALM.

I remember God capturing my attention at one point as I was talking this through with Him. He said, "Dianne, some of my kids are just so content being in the banquet room that they never even make it to their table. They never realize or see all that I have for them."

Immediately, tears flooded my eyes and a lump filled my throat. I totally got it. I understood. That room was so mesmerizing, so beautiful, so safe. I could have been super content just hanging out in the entryway. It was breathtaking and surreal. It was filled with a comfort and belonging I can't put into words.

I thought of myself and how I felt after I accepted Jesus. I was so thankful and overwhelmed with His beauty and presence, His saving grace, that I could have just stayed right there, in that safe spot, inside the doorway of the banquet room. I would have been so happy and blessed just to be invited in. Where I was before was so dark and burdensome; I had felt empty. One step in that box of beauty brought the utmost contentment.

I'm telling you, I never dreamed I should, let alone could, expect anything from my Heavenly Father. I was just thankful I was accepted by Him.

> I NEVER DREAMED I SHOULD, LET ALONE COULD, EXPECT ANYTHING FROM MY HEAVENLY FATHER. I WAS JUST THANKFUL I WAS ACCEPTED BY HIM.

But friends, that's not what God has for me or you. He doesn't have a "just get in the door" mentality. He says you and I are His. We are His kids, bought at the highest price. We are joint heirs with Jesus. Our Daddy is the King, and He wants us to take our full portion at the banquet table.

Yet, so many Christians are okay with just being in the room. I know; I was there for a very long time. It's easy to get distracted by the beauty of what God has invited us into that we never even notice that there is a whole banquet table piled high and overflowing with gifts made just for us. We each have our own table, our own gifts to unwrap one by one.

Friends, don't leave them there.

A few years ago, I was attending a business meeting where a dear friend was speaking. She used an illustration that has remained with me to this day. She was speaking to us about the opportunity that we all had to obtain financial increase in our industry. Every person in the room was given the opportunity through our company to earn a hefty bonus. The reality was not many of us had worked very hard for that bonus the previous month. Needless to say, very few earned it. She was there to help us understand the impact of our inadequacy and the impact of our contentment with the status quo. She wanted to challenge us and inspire us to go after all that was available to us.

She pulled out from under the podium a bag and started unloading stacks of hundred-dollar bills. I'm talking thousands of dollars. Her words and the stacks of cash sitting in front of me really drove the point home.

We all had the same incredible opportunity to earn the money that she laid out on the podium before us. The cash represented what was available for each us to receive. *What was I thinking? Why didn't I go after that? Why didn't I take what was available for me to take?*

Friends, listen to me; if you think that thousands of dollars of cash sitting on a table before you is motivating or inspiring, if that alone will challenge you to work harder, then imagine what God has sitting at the table He's prepared for you. It's there; it's all there, and it's not just financial.

It's spiritual, relational, and emotional.

It's healing, favor, blessing, and increase.

It's new opportunity and abundance.

It's more than you could ever think, dream, or imagine.

It's so much more than you could ever conceive.

But just like I had to be willing to work for my bonus, we must be willing to take a step forward. We can no longer be content with just getting in the doorway. We can't just go to church watch a service on TV, or listen to the latest and greatest podcast. All of that is good, but there is more available.

Friend, you have a calling, you have a purpose, you have a banquet table of gifts all wrapped up, beautifully tagged with your name on them. They're sitting there, untouched, waiting for you to step up and own them. No one else can have them; no one else is going to open them for you. You have to do it.

You have to move forward, stop being distracted, and dive into those gifts. You have to become all that you were created to be and experience all that God has created for you. Don't get to Heaven and have a whole table of gifts that were created just for you left untouched. Experience God's greatness now.

YOU HAVE A CALLING, YOU HAVE A PURPOSE, YOU HAVE A BANQUET TABLE OF GIFTS ALL WRAPPED UP, BEAUTIFULLY TAGGED WITH YOUR NAME ON THEM.

Imagine yourself going all out and getting those you love the most amazing gifts money could buy. Imagine searching high and low, finding the perfect treasures for each person. Now imagine having the ultimate spread for them to approach, each gift thought out intently and wrapped beautifully. Here you are, so excited, so pumped you can hardly stand it. You just want them to dive into them; you want to see their expression and know what they think. You long to see their smile as you sit on the edge of your seat in anticipation while they begin to unwrap each precious gift that you've thought of and prepared for them.

Now, imagine these loved ones of yours; imagine they enter that party room and never even approach the gift table. Imagine they never even take notice.

Or imagine that they see it but say, "Oh no, those couldn't possibly be for me. I don't deserve those."

I mean, imagine how our Creator, our Heavenly Father must feel. We, you and I, are His prized possessions, we are His kids, His children, and He has such greatness in store for each one of us. We just have to go and take what belongs to us.

We must expect that He has greatness for us, and that we can experience every ounce of it.

I believe with all my heart that God allowed me to see this vision, not just for me, but for you. I believe whole heartedly that there is a reason you are reading this book right now. You or someone you know needs this message.

I also believe the enemy wants nothing more than to keep you too distracted, too intimidated, too insecure to take action and approach your table with confidence.

He's terrified that you might realize all your heavenly Father has for you.

He's terrified of the power within you and the purpose you've been called to.

Go after your gifts, my friends. Don't be like me. I was sitting in a meeting room listening to one of the most beautiful, inspiring, talented, and successful friends and mentors speak, throwing all of my opportunity out on the table before me, knowing it was too late to do anything about it.

> DON'T SPEND ANOTHER SECOND OF YOUR LIFE STANDING IN THE DOORWAY. USE THE TOOLS AND TRUTHS WE'VE TALKED ABOUT TO SHATTER THE WALL THAT IS STOPPING YOU FROM SEEING AND RECEIVING WHAT HAS ALWAYS BEEN YOURS!

Don't spend another second of your life standing in the doorway. Use the tools and truths we've talked about to shatter the wall that is stopping you from seeing and receiving what has always been yours!

DON'T LET GOOD GET IN THE WAY OF GREAT

Is it possible that some of us, wall or no wall, might be distracted? Distracted by Christian contentment? Sidetracked by the good and not going after the great?

I'm convinced that one of the most used tactics of the Enemy is distraction. If he can keep you distracted, he knows he can keep you from God's greatness. If you're content with standing in the doorway, he doesn't have to worry about you stepping over the threshold, into the banquet room, and up to your table to take what's yours.

You'll never know authority is yours for the taking if you don't go unwrap it. Healing will hold no power unless you go get it, faithfully believing it to be true. Your gifts of wisdom, understanding, new relationships, restoration, and financial breakthrough will never be opened and experienced.

It's critical that you know and work towards the plan and purpose

God has for you. He does not intend for us to merely enter a relationship him, say we believe in Him but never go beyond that. We must invite Him in to our marriage to open the gift of what He can do in our marriage. We must invite Him and walk with Him into our finances to access the gift of what He can do in our finances. We must go take what is ours. We must break through the barrier of distraction and insecurity. That's what He wants us to do. Stop being timid and wondering if you deserve it. Just go for it.

None of us deserve the righteousness of God or any of these beautiful gifts, but because of the blood of Jesus, we get access to them all. Accept that and move, go, do, be all you were created to be.

I'm overwhelmed with joy as I type these words. I mean, can you imagine what this world would be if each of us approached our banquet table and accepted everything on it? Can you imagine the favor we would be walking in, the authority, the purpose, the passion, the opportunities, the open doors, the divine appointments? Can you fathom the mentors and life-giving relationships that God has packaged for us? The ministry, the opportunities we will get to be His hands and feet, the work we will be blessed to be a part of, the dreams that will become realities, the impossible that will become possible?

My heart is exploding. Friends, go right now; go get them.

Don't wait; don't be distracted, not even by the good. Do whatever you have to do to get to where you need to be.

Don't let clutter, busyness, or people get in your way. Don't let that stuff hold you back.

Get up early. Study the Word of God; study it like you've never heard it. Learn it and unlearn some of what you have been taught. Believe God's Word to be true for you. Ask the Holy Spirit to invade you and consume your thoughts. Speak life and expect God's greatness.

STUDY THE WORD OF GOD; STUDY IT LIKE YOU'VE NEVER HEARD IT.

Greatness?

It can't be measured or fully explained. So much of it makes little sense to the human mind, logic becomes the laughing stock in comparison. Even those who deny it now will one day confess it to be true. It's exemplified in everything we see and in everything we don't. It's found in each breath we take and in every moment that passes by. It's been present since the beginning of time and will exist through all eternity. Great minds have tried to pack it in to eloquent quotes, and some theorists have tried to debate its truth. Yet it stands, untouchable yet tangible, solid yet gentle, tough yet tender. It goes far beyond our ability to comprehend, yet it's lived out through each and every living being including you and me. It's mesmerizing and unfathomable, full of beauty. It's possibilities will most likely be wrapped in what seems to be the impossible. It's absolutely fascinating, and every ounce of it is available to you, all of it.

If you haven't figured it out, I'm referring to the greatness of God.

I mentioned earlier how God spoke to me about teaching His kids to expect His greatness. I did the best I knew how to do at the moment I heard Him speak it over me. I simply began to study it and expect it for myself, but over time, God began to expect more out of me.

I've shared so much of my story, but the most fascinating part of all of it is the outrageous love of God. He loves us so much. I know you've heard this; I know you've probably experienced this, but His love, His grace, and His mercy are just too good. The crazy thing is, there are people we rub shoulders with every day that don't know this truth. They don't know Jesus. They are God's children but don't know it yet. They haven't accepted the gift of His salvation.

Once people get a glimpse of God and all His glory, they'll be rocked by His giant tsunami wave of mercy, love, and compassion. We can't keep this to ourselves. Friends, we have to share it; we must live His love so loud that it makes people stop and wonder what's different. We must be filled with the joy of the Lord. We need to walk around confident of our call, covered in His peace and overflowing with His Spirit.

WE MUST LIVE HIS LOVE SO LOUD THAT IT MAKES PEOPLE STOP AND WONDER WHAT'S DIFFERENT.

He loves us. We don't deserve it; we can't earn it. We can hardly comprehend it, but it is there, this love that is almost unexplainable because of its perfection and purity. There is nothing like it in the whole world.

We need to shout it from the rooftops. Not necessarily verbally, but in how we live, speak, walk, and act, through our integrity and our unwavering faith and confidence in the fact that we are His, and He is ours.

Together, let's show people how special we are to Him. Let's display what it looks like to be a child of the King. He loves you and me individually, as if we were the only one here. It's not abnormal for Him to whisper special things to each of us or encourage our faith in unique ways that mean so much to us individually. We are not a mass production; we weren't created on an assembly line. His love is individual, specific, and purposeful. It's perfect.

He never leaves us. He never forsakes us. He'll never leave you stranded or backs out at the last minute. He'll always shows up because He's always there. As matter of fact, you can't escape Him even if you try.

WE ARE NOT A MASS PRODUCTION; WE WEREN'T CREATED ON AN ASSEMBLY LINE. HIS LOVE IS INDIVIDUAL, SPECIFIC, AND PURPOSEFUL. IT'S PERFECT.

Romans 8:38-39 (NLT) says,

"And I am convinced that nothing can ever separate us from God's love. Neither death nor life, neither angels nor demons, neither our fears for today nor our worries about tomorrow—not even the powers of hell can separate us from God's love. No power in the sky above or in the earth below—indeed, nothing in all creation will ever be able to separate us from the love of God that is revealed in Christ Jesus our Lord."

In my darkest moments when I felt furthest from Him, I knew He was right there. I knew He was beckoning me home. I'm so thankful for that. He loves us too much to leave us. He will fight for us. He will never stop seeking us out. We may feel alone in the crowd, but He has His eyes fixed on His baby girl, on His boy. You're never unseen.

His heart hurts when ours does. He knows and holds every tear we shed. He knows when we're happy and when we feel crushed. He

YOU'RE NEVER UNSEEN.

sees our deepest thoughts and our greatest fears. He knows exactly what we need and exactly when we need it. His greatness cannot be explained by words, although some of the most poetic can help us fathom a bit of it.

He is God, and we are His.

Here's a dialogue that God and I have quite often. I mentioned it earlier, but maybe it can help you.

When something seems too big, too scary, too much, I will often hear Him whisper.

"Dianne, whose are you?"

And I in return will say, "I am Yours."

His reply is always, "And who am I?"

I will respond, "You are God."

Then, He says this, "And is anything impossible for me?"

Once again, He puts into perspective with His soft whisper just how great He is and who exactly I am.

I am His. Yes! I am the daughter of God Almighty, the Creator of the heavens and the earth, the one for whom nothing is too big, and nothing is impossible. He is mine, and I long to share Him with the world because everybody deserves a daddy like that.

Here's the deal: I feel completely, outrageously, undoubtedly unqualified to even write the things I'm writing. There are so many who have greater knowledge and theological backgrounds. There are those with much more wisdom and understanding. I have no "Bible" school background; I'm a stay- at-home mom with an associate degree from a local community college, which I'm not at all going to downplay because I earned that baby, and I'm proud of it. Just sayin'!

But here's what I do have. I have a life flipped upside down and inside out by the radical love of Jesus.

I have fallen madly in love with my Creator.

I have never, ever been failed by Him. He is constant and true. He is always there; He's my greatest cheerleader and biggest kick in the pants. He loves me, He adores me, and I absolutely, wholeheartedly adore Him, too. I may not have a seminary background, but I have a background, one that has taught me the greatest lesson I can learn.

I am His, and He is mine. I am the daughter of the King, and that King is my daddy!

> WE MUST UNDERSTAND THAT WE ARE LOVED DESPITE OUR INADEQUACIES AND FAILINGS.

It's so important that we really get this; it's like critically important. It's one of the greatest of God's gifts. We must understand that we are LOVED despite our inadequacies and failings. Friends, this truth, this gift is so HUGE. It positions us to love others, even though they may fail us. When we open up the gift of unconditional love, only then can we really love others.

THAT'S A WRAP

We've walked through a lot of things together throughout the pages of this book. Mostly it's a lot of my story, but my heart's cry is that it helps you in your journey, in your walk with God. Earlier in this book, we talked about a passage from Isaiah. It's found in Isaiah 61:3 and part of that verse goes something like this:

God is going to give you beauty for your ashes, joy for your mourning, and a garment (a covering) of praise for your heaviness. (paraphrased)

Most of you have been through more than most people know. You carry things that are heavy and burdensome, and most of you probably keep it buried down deep inside, just dealing with it, carrying the weight of your wall. Hear me when I say this, YOU DON'T HAVE TO CARRY ANY OF IT ANY LONGER. There is beauty for your ashes.

He's got you.

So, don't be ashamed of your ashes, your mourning, or your heaviness. All that hurt will turn into beauty, joy, and praise. Tell

DON'T BE ASHAMED OF YOUR ASHES, YOUR MOURNING, OR YOUR HEAVINESS. ALL THAT HURT WILL TURN INTO BEAUTY, JOY, AND PRAISE.

others about your wall and how you shattered it with truth. There is power in your testimony. Show them that they, too, may experience beauty from their ashes.

See your wall my friends. Break it down, shatter that sucker.

Take what's yours and begin to expect and experience God's greatness.

God has provided every tool we need to accomplish this. His Word being our number one weapon.

> THE WORD OF GOD IS ALIVE AND ACTIVE; IT'S A WEAPON OF DESTRUCTION WHEN SPOKEN IN FAITH OVER THE LIES OF THE ENEMY.

Hebrews 4:12 (NIV) says,

"For the word of God is alive and active. Sharper than any double-edged sword, it penetrates even to dividing soul and spirit, joints and marrow; it judges the thoughts and attitudes of the heart."

Remember, the Word of God is alive and active; it's a weapon of destruction when spoken in faith over the lies of the Enemy. We simply need to use the Word of God to shatter our walls. Speak His truth, and it will penetrate any wall that stands in your way. Literally speak God's truth out loud over your situation. Five of my favorites that I declare daily are:

For I know the plans you have for me, plans for a hope and a future. (Jeremiah 29:11)

By His stripes I am healed. (Isaiah 53:5)

I can do all things through Christ who strengthens me. (Philippians 4:13)

The devil flees me because I resist him in the name of Jesus. (James 4:7)

I am the righteousness of God through Christ Jesus. (5:21)

There are literally hundreds of scriptures that you can claim and speak over your life, your gifts.

These are just a handful of my favorites.

One of the greatest blessings I've had the privilege of receiving is the understanding of who I truly am in Christ. It was life changing. It completely revolutionized everything, from the way I talk, think, speak and even complete daily tasks. It has flipped my world upside down, and I know it's just the beginning of all He has for me. The same is for you; dive in and unwrap all that God has prepared. Start, if you haven't already, by learning who you truly are, understanding the heart of your Father, giving yourself permission to expect great things from Him. Rip into the gift of authenticity, and oh, don't forget the precious gift of learning His voice. My heart's cry is that you would begin to understand that you are truly loved, adored, and favored more than you could ever possibly imagine; that you

> THIS WALL-BREAKING, GIFT-OPENING JOURNEY IS BY FAR THE MOST EXHILARATING, EXCITING, AND LIFE CHANGING PROCESS YOU WILL EVER EXPERIENCE. ONLY TO BE TRUMPED BY THE SALVATION OFFERED THROUGH JESUS HIMSELF.

were made on purpose, for a purpose. God has great things for you to do, people to impact, love, and serve. He has healing and provision, relationships and restoration; he has so much waiting for you to discover. I can't even image what else lies inside the unwrapped gifts that are yet to be opened. This wall-breaking, gift-opening journey is by far the most exhilarating, exciting, and life changing process you will ever experience. Only to be trumped by the Salvation offered through Jesus Himself.

You are gifted, my friends, in ways you never dreamed or dared to be possible. Refuse to let all that belongs to you sit any longer.

Expect God's greatness in your life.

Take the plunge; I dare you.

Cannonball it.

Shatter the walls that stand before you and take all that's been prepared for you.

Go get your great!

SHATTER THE WALLS THAT STAND BEFORE YOU
AND TAKE ALL THAT'S BEEN PREPARED FOR YOU.

GO GET YOUR GREAT!

ACKNOWLEDGEMENTS

To the two human beings that make me want to live my life better each and every day, Nevaeh and Braden. My prayer is that the two of you chase down every dream in your heart and to love Jesus with all that you are while doing so. If ever a wall stands in your way, may this guide you in shattering the crap out of that sucker. I love you more than you will ever know. Change the world, my loves. You've got everything you need to do it!

To my husband and love of my life, Don: You are one in a million. Thank you for loving me, encouraging me, and inspiring me every single day. Life is an adventure with you and so much fun… thank you for loving me as you do. I love you.

Mom: Thank you for being my ladder. You'll understand when you read chapter 5. I love you! To my family: This year has been tough, but God is good, and as Dad said, "Everything is gonna be alright!"

Amber: Thank you for saying yes and stepping into all that God has called you to. You're changing the world, my friend. I'm so thankful for you and your friendship.

To the UHP team: You are all rockstars. Thank you for pouring endless hours into this project and for making me sound better than I am. I love you all! It's been such a joy working with you.

To every woman who feels this call, this desire in the depth of her heart to be more. That's greatness inside of you, and it's bubbling up. Don't hold it in. Let it out, girl! Read the Word, study it, live it, grow in it, even when you don't fully get it, just keep reading, studying, and spending time with God. It's in those moments when you choose to let the truth of God simmer in your heart and mind that His greatness will explode inside of you, pouring out in your words, thoughts, and actions. Suddenly it will begin to immerse those around you, and little-by-little, day-by-day, you will begin changing the world even more than you already are. I'm cheering you on my friends.

ABOUT THE AUTHOR

Dianne Wyper is many things to many people, but to all, she is the Jesus-loving girl next door. As a writer, speaker, and worship leader, Dianne longs to help women reclaim their true identity. She believes that by equipping women in truth and encouraging them in love, she may see the women of God take their place and step into their calling, becoming all they were created to be.

As a wife, mother, and friend, Dianne likes to keep her home in Michigan full of people. She loves to cultivate God's greatness in each heart that comes through her home by using her creativity and warm gatherings to inspire honest conversation about Jesus.

As a self-proclaimed atmosphere junkie, she also believes firmly in plenty of good coffee, great food, and laughter. When Dianne isn't spending time with her husband and two kiddos, or diving into a new project or book, you can find her encouraging others through one of her many other outlets.

To learn more about Dianne, visit her website:
www.DianneWyper.com.

STAY CONNECTED WITH DIANNE

DianneWyper.com
Instagram @diannewyper